Quarterly Essay

CW00539472

Quarterly Essay is published four times a year by Black Inc., an imprint of Schwartz Books Pty Ltd. Publisher: Morry Schwartz.

ISBN 9781760641528 ISSN 1832-0953

ALL RIGHTS RESERVED.

Subscriptions – 1 year print & digital (4 issues): $79.95 within Australia incl. GST. Outside Australia $119.95. 2 years print & digital (8 issues): $149.95 within Australia incl. GST. 1 year digital only: $49.95.

Payment may be made by Mastercard or Visa, or by cheque made out to Schwartz Books. Payment includes postage and handling.

To subscribe, fill out and post the subscription form inside this issue, or subscribe online:

quarterlyessay.com
subscribe@blackincbooks.com
Phone: 61 3 9486 0288

Correspondence should be addressed to:

The Editor, Quarterly Essay
Level 1, 221 Drummond Street
Carlton VIC 3053 Australia
Phone: 61 3 9486 0288 / Fax: 61 3 9011 6106
Email: quarterlyessay@blackincbooks.com

Editor: Chris Feik. Management: Elisabeth Young. Publicity: Anna Lensky. Design: Guy Mirabella. Assistant Editor: Kirstie Innes-Will. Production Coordinator: Marilyn de Castro. Typesetting: Akiko Chan.

Printed in Australia by McPherson's Printing Group. The paper used to produce this book comes from wood grown in sustainable forests.

MEN AT WORK

Australia's parenthood trap

Annabel Crabb

In May 2018, a child was born. It seemed – from what I could tell, allowing for the array of crocheted blankets in which it was swaddled – a very sweet but otherwise unremarkable infant. Two button eyes, a nose, probably bipedal, and so on. And yet this was one of the most celebrated and controversial children the Southern Hemisphere has encountered this decade.

Why? Because her mother is the serving prime minister of New Zealand.

Baby Neve's mother, Jacinda Ardern, was hammered during the October 2017 election campaign with questions on her specific intentions vis-à-vis the biological equipment with which she – at birth – had been endowed and which in her thirty-seven years she had yet to engage fully in pursuit of her biological destiny. And when she finally announced her pregnancy – well. All bets were off. In Australia, she became the most remarkable New Zealander since Russell Crowe, or Phar Lap. No matter that Ms Ardern was not even the only New Zealand–born political leader to make a baby that year (the Australian deputy prime minister, Barnaby Joyce, having unexpectedly shared line honours in that respect). As the New Zealand prime ministerial ankles swelled, so did the column inches of advice, congratulation and condemnation extended to this woman on a mission which – as readers were tirelessly reminded – no woman had attempted since Benazir Bhutto. (And look what happened to her.) From Angela Shanahan, at *The Australian*:

> There are the simple practical issues: the three- to four-hourly feeds for which, being a greenie leftie, she will try to do using her own milk; the sleepless nights, which reduce many women to a zombie-like state; and the blithe confidence that after six weeks her partner will take over as full-time caregiver. Well, good luck with that one, too, because the father is not the mother and there is such a thing as maternal bonding, which is a basic post-partum physical need for mothers and infants. This woman needs at least six months off, not six weeks.

On both sides of the Tasman, the logistics of Ardern's post-partum schedule were a question on which everyone, it seemed, had an urgent opinion.

A little over a year later, the Liberal Party of Australia – in one of its increasingly customary leadership coups – tipped out the serving prime minister, Malcolm Turnbull, and his deputy, Julie Bishop, and replaced them with Scott Morrison and Josh Frydenberg. Morrison and Frydenberg were something of an ecclesiastical first. The nation had never had a Pentecostal prime minister before, let alone one serving with a Jewish deputy and treasurer. Morrison immediately made the crippling national drought his primary concern, advocating prayer for rain; two days after his elevation, Bourke Airport recorded its highest single-day rainfall on record, suggesting that – in Bourke at least – the Almighty may have had an ear pricked. But there was something else unusual about the pair. Not since the mid-1970s, when Malcolm Fraser appointed a young John Howard to be his treasurer, had these two positions been held by the fathers of young children. Morrison's daughters, Abbey and Lily, were both at primary school. Frydenberg's kids were even younger: Gemma a pre-schooler, Blake a toddler.

One can only imagine the sustained national heart attack that would have accompanied the appointment of two *mothers* of young children to these demanding jobs. And we do need to rely on our imaginations, as no woman with children of any age has ever served as prime minister, or treasurer, or indeed as deputy leader of the Liberal or Labor parties in government. However, the first joint press conference given by the two men came and went without anyone raising the question that almost certainly would have been the first asked at an all-mothers affair: "How are you going to manage it all?"

Now, this essay isn't going to be a lengthy whine about how life is tough for Jacinda Ardern and easy for Scott Morrison. I'd never argue that. But parliament is – in many respects – a brightly lit model village of our national sentiment. It's an absolutely intriguing demonstration of what we expect from fathers that the question of work–family balance – for a parent with the biggest job in the country – *doesn't even come up*. For three weeks, Morrison and Frydenberg were interviewed about everything from faith to football to their favourite songs. I tweeted my observation about both of them having young families and was immediately accused by some anonymous snarler of "trying to humanise them." Right, I thought. I can hardly complain about nobody asking them how they are going to manage things if I can't be bothered to do it myself. So I called them both.

And the first thing that became obvious was how unaccustomed each of these men was to considering this question. Working mothers of any public profile or professional seniority are asked how they "manage it all" with such lavish regularity that their answer is like a little psalm they know by heart. Here's mine: "Well. Mondays Jeremy works half a day from home, so that's my day of working like a normal person. Thursday and Friday the kids are at after-school care, Tuesday and Wednesday are a crapshoot; sometimes I'll come home from work for school pick-up and go back to work after they're in bed, or hit up the favour bank, which – in my neighbourhood of school parents – is a busy institution of daily withdrawals and deposits. (I'll pick your kid up from piano on Tuesday if you'll take mine to gymnastics Wednesday. I've got a vat of bolognese sauce to feed ten kids if you'll look after mine for a few hours from three.) I do most of the cooking; Jem does grocery shopping, laundry and school forms. Some days it all works smoothly. Some days it's a debacle."

Working mothers are so used to comparing notes on how they manage it all that it's practically a language. But what I realised quickly when talking to the prime minister and treasurer was that they are not fluent. Here's what the treasurer said:

> Whenever I am away, we use FaceTime a lot, and whenever I am at home I do stories, milk and bed, and try to play as much ball sports and Lego as possible. Running races at the park [is] also a regular. We always have Friday night together as a family meal, which is always special.

And here's the prime minister:

> The first point is that none of this would be possible without the kids having an amazing mum. That's true for me and for Josh. But it's about priorities. Little rituals are important. You've got to talk every day and we try to do it twice a day. We do FaceTime when we can. Little things, like: 'Where are you today?' You hold the camera phone up and you show them where you are. My kids have grown up while I was in politics and I think that's a good thing, on balance, because life is more normal to them. Jen and the girls almost never come to Canberra. We have our friends and our family that we socialise with and they're very disconnected from the world of politics. It means our kids are growing up in a normal environment and that's very important to us.

With both men, I had to rephrase the question several times to explain what I was getting at: "How does it work? How do you manage, day to day?" And what became clear was that both their models were about coping with or compensating for absence. FaceTiming every day or dining together once a week is an expression of parental love and devotion – and very important it is too – but it doesn't contribute much practical horse-power to the engine that keeps a family running. Who does school pick-ups? Who remembers to take them to the dentist? What happens when they're sick? Their spouses do most of that stuff.

And while handing over the lion's share of parenting to a spouse is the stuff of international headlines when it's Jacinda Ardern, when it's Scott Morrison it's so unremarkable as to occasion no comment whatsoever.

Now, I would never question the love or commitment of either man to his children; both Scott Morrison and Josh Frydenberg are exceptionally besotted with and close to their kids. What I want to know is: why do we expect so little of fathers? Why do we fret so extensively about the impact on children of not seeing their mothers enough, but care so little about what happens when it's Dad who's always away? Do we think dads are just for weekends? Or are we simply so roundly prepared – based on what we see – for their absence that we neither mourn it nor remark on it?

In August 2014, the Silicon Valley executive Max Schireson wrote a fas-cinating blog post. He was the CEO of his own madly successful enterprise, but used his personal blog to announce that he was stepping down because constant travel made it impossible to spend enough time with his three young children. The stress of constant separation was – for him – the big-gest issue in his life, and he was mystified that in all the press attention he received, this was the one question that was never asked of him:

> As a male CEO, I have been asked what kind of car I drive and what type of music I like, but never how I balance the demands of being both a dad and a CEO. While the press haven't asked me, it is a ques-tion that I often ask myself. Here is my situation:
>
> I have three wonderful kids at home, aged 14, 12 and 9, and I love spending time with them: skiing, cooking, playing back-gammon, swimming, watching movies or Warriors or Giants games, talking, whatever.

I am on pace to fly 300,000 miles this year, all the normal CEO travel plus commuting between Palo Alto and New York every two to three weeks. During that travel, I have missed a lot of family fun, perhaps more importantly, I was not with my kids when our puppy was hit by a car, or when my son had (minor and success-ful, and of course unexpected) emergency surgery.

I have an amazing wife who also has an important career; she is a doctor and professor at Stanford ... I love her; I am forever in her debt for finding a way to keep the family working despite my crazy travel. I should not continue abusing that patience.

I'd always been quietly enraged by the interviews with female CEOs that start with the question of how they manage their families along with their jobs. But reading Schireson's post made me change my mind completely. Now I don't get mad when female leaders are asked that ques-tion. It's a bloody sensible question. Now I just get mad when male leaders aren't asked it. Not asking is actually, in itself, quite a powerful message. It says, "No one expects you to care about this." It says, "It's not your job to worry about that stuff." It says, "Whatever efforts you do make, or whatever private griefs your big job cloaks, are not of interest to anyone." And for an increasing number of young fathers who do want to live their lives differently from the way their own fathers did, that's an insult.

It's an antiquated view of what fatherhood is. But it's a view that is rein-forced every day, at all levels of Australian society, at both a formal and a casual level. From the moment that sperm hits egg, we treat mothers as the proper parents and fathers as their gormless accessories. We have a national paid parental leave scheme for the primary caregiver, and an ancillary mini-scheme for the other parent. We have "mothers' groups" for the parents of babies. We have the term "working mum" for a mother who works, as if that's special enough to be surprising. But "working dad" isn't a thing people say.

Half a century of modern feminism has changed the way women conduct their lives almost beyond recognition. But men are still in their old box. And the risk implicit in this arrangement is bigger than just insulting a generation of fathers who want to do things differently. This is an age in which the #MeToo movement has pricked the world's ears to the stories of women. In which some large organisations adopt formal programs geared to increasing the number of women in leadership positions. Young men arrive in these workplaces who have never sexually harassed anyone, and yet feel the uneasy legacy of Harvey Weinstein and his ilk. These young men have commonly been outperformed at school and university by their female peers, and yet may find their new workplaces have schemes in place to increase the rates at which women are hired or promoted. How galling is it for this generation of men (who, as we shall see, are keen to be more involved with their children than their own fathers were) to find that flexible work and parental leave are still options reserved largely for women? Discrimination against men in the area of parenting is commonplace; it's even – as I shall explain – sanctioned by Commonwealth law. And this discrimination underpins ancient structures that disadvantage not only men, but women and children too.

In this essay, I want to do something that's isn't done enough: look squarely at men and how they work, and how their working lives change – or rather, don't change – when they become fathers. Too often, gender equity in workplaces is just a debate about what happens to women. How many of them get promoted, what the barriers are, and so on. But what about the expectations that the workplace imposes on fathers? What are the invisible rules that prevent men from seeking flexible work and parental leave the way women do? This is a worthwhile question just for men's sake, and for the sake of their children. But it's also worth asking for women's sake. Because, of course, so long as women and men continue to hook up and make babies together, the way men work and live will be a significant constituent element of the choices that women are able to make.

So let's go back to New Zealand for a moment and broaden our gaze. For all the headlines about Jacinda Ardern, the person who made it possible for her to serve as a rare breastfeeding world leader is – to a significant extent – her husband, Clarke Gayford, who was named in the role of primary carer when the NZ prime minister's pregnancy was announced. And so it was that Mr Gayford – formerly the genial and unnecessarily handsome presenter of a fishing program – shuffled into the most conflicted occupation a modern man can attempt: the Stay-at-Home Dad.

I call it the Hero–Zero complex. On one hand, the Stay-at-Home Dad tends to be lionised. Often by women, who are so intensely thrilled by the idea of a bloke who would shoulder responsibility for remembering whose birthday party it is on Saturday and whether it's Mufti Day tomorrow that they actually want to touch the guy, not in a sexy way but just to make sure he's real. The congratulation of the Stay-at-Home Dad in such circles can be over the top. Crazy. Hyper-excitable. Which is unfortunate, because then the Zero factor kicks in. This is where the Stay-at-Home Dad is treated as though he has ceased to exist, or has chosen a way of life of no significance whatsoever. Typically, this treatment comes from former workmates who stop inviting him to things and, when they do run into him, say awkward things like "Still being Mister Mum, then?" or "So when are you coming back to work?"

Were he a woman, Clarke Gayford would be unremarkable. He'd join the dignified ranks of political spouses who for centuries have attended school plays with plenty of room on the neighbouring seat to store their handbags. But he's a fellow, so his Hero–Zero complex kicked in pretty fast once the happy news of the pregnancy was announced. He swiftly felt the ugly undertow of what happens, in this social media age, when men and women do the reverse of what underlying gender expectations silently but powerfully command them to do. More or less immediately, a subterranean online gossip campaign engulfed the man, so intensely that the couple were obliged to protest publicly. Conspiracy websites canvassed everything from Mr Gayford's alleged excessive partying to the proposal that Ms Ardern was a notorious transsexual who was faking her pregnancy. You might laugh, or at least raise a sceptical eyebrow. But entire books have been written about the theory that Sarah Palin faked her pregnancy in the 2008 US election campaign. Some people take this sort of stuff seriously. And in Mr Gayford's case, we can wearily recognise some of the treatment handed out to Peter Davis, the spouse of New Zealand's preceding female prime minister, who for decades was accused of being a front for his wife's lesbianism. Or indeed to Tim Mathieson, the spouse of Australia's first female prime minister, who also was accused (accurately) of being a hairdresser and (inaccurately) of being a front for his partner's lesbianism, and asked publicly by a radio presenter whether it was true that he was gay. (This fascination with Tim Mathieson's occupation as a hairdresser always confounded me. My firm view has always been that a woman who needs to be TV-ready by 6 a.m. most mornings and who hooks up with a hairdresser is crazy like a fox.)

It is at once extraordinary and predictable the way public figures can be punished for violating the roles that their gender recommends they play. And it's also extraordinary how unoriginal those punishments are, from country to country. It gives us a sniff of what sort of attitudes might meet ordinary men who take on the role of stay-at-home fathering and are not married to a world leader.

This seems a good moment to check how many such men there are. In the past decade, there's been quite a bit of chat about stay-at-home dads. There's been a popular TV show featuring handsome SAHDs. There have been articles, think-pieces, support groups, days of action – all sorts. And yet the actual number of stay-at-home dads in Australia remains stubbornly stagnant. About 4 per cent of Australian families with kids under eighteen had stay-at-home fathers in 1991. These days, according to the latest census, it's 5 per cent. So we've ticked up one percentage point in twenty-five years. Barely a change; for all the talk, stay-at-home dads are still the black swan of parents.

But plenty else has changed over that time. For instance, the proportion of stay-at-home mums has decreased from 33 per cent to 27 per cent. And the proportion of households with both parents out of work has decreased from 12 per cent to 7 per cent. Where's everyone gone? "To work" is the answer. Between 1991 and 2016, the proportion of family households in which both parents work rose from 52 per cent to 61 per cent. Two-income families are now the norm.

More parents working should – you'd think – generate a new round of juggling as parents thrash out new ways of ensuring kids are fed, bathed, played with and ferried to and from school around work hours. And you'd be right. But it's mothers, by and large, who are taking up the slack.

This essay won't be heavy on the graphs, but there's one you *really* need to see if you want the baldest possible visual demonstration of how differently mothers and fathers experience work–family balance. It was composed by Jenny Baxter, a researcher at the Australian Institute of Family Studies. When Baxter first unveiled it at a conference, the audience audibly gasped. The right-hand figure shows what happens to a woman's life in the first twelve years after becoming a mother. At birth, her parenting hours shoot up – quite understandably – from zero to about forty-five hours a week. This workload tapers steadily away over the following twelve years. Her paid work hours plummet, and she gradually builds them back up over the ensuing decade, although she never quite ends up back where she started. And on the birth of the child, her time spent on housework abruptly doubles, and stays that way. I look at the sharp peaks, surges and reversals that characterise this graph and I recognise in it the feeling of balancing the care of very young children with a full-time job. The graph itself looks like the heart rate of a very, very stressed person.

However, if you look at the accompanying chart – the mean hours per week spent by fathers of young children on paid work, housework and child care – it's an entirely different matter. Time spent on parenting rises

Figure 1: Father's and mother's time use up to and after the birth of first child

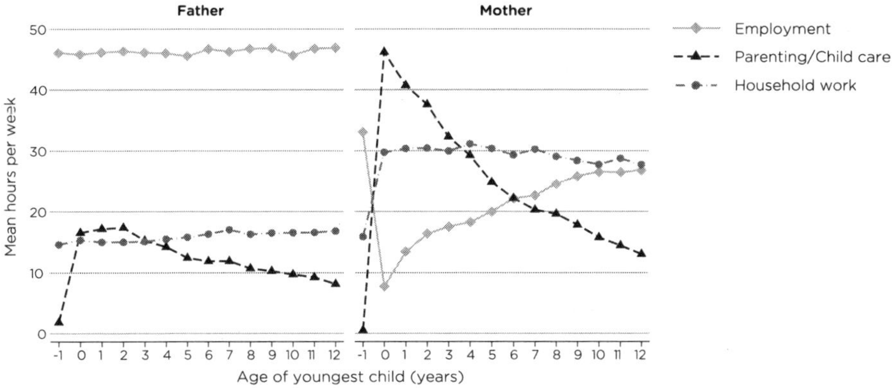

Source: Commonwealth of Australia, CC By 4.0

with the birth of the child, although not – again, understandably – to the level of a mother. But it's the other two indicators that are absolutely astounding. Mean hours spent on housework barely shift for men with the birth of a baby. A man will, generally speaking, do about fifteen hours a week of domestic work before the birth of his child, and around fifteen hours a week after, for the first twelve years of that child's life. And his hours of paid work forge along at forty-five hours a week, blithely unaffected by the significant change in his personal circumstances.

In other words, when a family changes, it is women who change and adapt to the new reality. Why not men?

*

Quite reasonably, the focus of the transformative feminist movement over the past half-century has been on the elimination of barriers to women in the workplace, from the establishment of anti-discrimination and affirmative action laws to the development of paid maternity leave. We've tried mentoring schemes, targets, consciousness-raising retreats and much else to boost women's participation at work, and yet still inhabit a country in which women are 60 per cent of university graduates and 45 per cent of middle managers, yet only 10 per cent of executives and 6 per cent of CEOs in the ASX200. And yes, there are more men called Andrew in that cohort than there are women, as is regularly observed.

It is perfectly normal, under these circumstances, for us to keep up our efforts and continue paying attention to what happens to women in the workplace. But as long as women keep making babies with men, then we are kidding ourselves if we continue to ignore the other side of the equation. Which is: what happens to men in the workplace. More specifically, what happens to men when they have kids.

It's well established that having children is entirely different, when it comes to your professional outlook, depending on whether you're male or female. I'm yet to find a more graphic piece of number-crunching on this than the famous NATSEM modelling I cited in my 2014 book *The Wife Drought*. NATSEM calculated that a 25-year-old man embarking on an average forty-year career can expect to earn $2 million over the course of that career. If he has kids, that goes up to $2.5 million. A woman of the same age and aptitude, setting out on the same career, can expect to earn $1.9 million. But if she has kids, that goes down to $1.3 million. Any study you like in this area will show you that the same biological event – reproduction – means strikingly different things for men at work as opposed to women. While motherhood tends to jam a stick in the spokes of a woman's marketability in the workplace, fatherhood is consistent with greater employability, greater perceived reliability and increased likelihood of promotion.

Why would this seemingly bizarre deviation occur, among men and women who are similarly qualified, similarly ambitious and experiencing similar life events? Well, as we have seen, it's because workplace expectations are so hugely different between the genders. When a woman has a baby, our society and the vast majority of workplaces are geared to expect – accurately, by and large – that she will be primarily responsible for the care and supervision of that baby. When that baby gets sick, it is she who will stay home from work. And when that baby gets older and the school needs volunteers for the Book Parade or the canteen, it is she who will somehow find some time and headspace to help out. Of a man who has a child, however, our system actively assumes that he has a wife who will look after all of those things. And he will thus experience all of the work-compatible elements of parenthood – the sobering sense of new responsibility, the stability, the sense of being a grown-up – without any of the attention-sapping, messy bits. Parenthood makes men into even more ideal employees, and women into less ideal ones.

Now, you can interpret this matrix of assumptions as hugely unfair to women, and I do. But it's also unfair to men. It simply dismisses the idea that men might be interested in being involved with their children. And it creates horrible fear and apprehension among men who would like to arrange their lives differently. And while this may not win the gold medal in the Injustice Olympics, it is an injustice that has significant and rippling consequences. Because the inability of a father to work flexibly, or leave when he needs to, creates a parallel obligation for someone else – usually a woman – to pick up the slack.

This lopsided pattern – that having a family makes a man more success-ful, and a woman less so – only really works if fathers behave as we expect them to behave. That is, as if having children has had no impact on their lives at all. Women suffer professionally when the model holds. But men suffer in other ways. A 2013 study of middle-class workers in Canada found that "caregiving" fathers were subjected to more mistreatment at work than traditional fathers, and in some workplaces more than twice as much mistreatment as "caregiving" mothers. Of the women studied, those without children were hassled more than mothers. In fact, patterns of mis-treatment – the researchers found – were much more to do with how closely workers conformed to traditional expectations than they were to do with gender on its own. The least mistreated people tended to be men who had children but did not take anything beyond customary responsibility for them, and women who had children and did. Those in line for a tougher time were women without children, who were thought cold or indifferent, and men looking after their children, who were thought soft.

This totally gels with what I've observed of the political workplace. Men without kids are problematic: Bob Carr, for instance, of whom it was famously said by John Hewson that you had to be suspicious of a guy who didn't drive and didn't like kids. Men with kids are ideal for politics, as long as they're prepared not to spend too much time with them. Mr Carr's successor, Morris Iemma, had four children, but was seriously criticised for lacking commitment to the job because he insisted on getting home to see them before bedtime once or twice a week. Gladys Berejiklian, shortly after becoming premier, was asked if she thought her childlessness would prevent her understanding the lives of ordinary citizens. And ask any female MP who has children how often she gets hate mail about being a bad mother. It's not that women in politics are punished for having children. It's more complicated than that. They're punished for not behaving – as mothers – in the way we expect them to. It's the breach of the expectation, rather than the circumstance itself: doing jobs you're not supposed to do, or not doing jobs that you are supposed to do. Said Barnaby Joyce, in one of his interviews after the birth of his new son: "I think people [would be] surprised [that] when I am home I do all the cooking, I do the washing, hang things out, clean around the house. I find it, I know it sounds weird, cathartic." Well, why would that be weird? That a person who's just had a baby would do cooking and washing and cleaning and hanging things out?

On the other side of the register, it's also thought weird – even actionable – when a woman tries to outsource the very same kind of work that is so surprisingly pleasurable to Mr Joyce. I hesitate to wade very deeply into the waters of The People vs Emma Husar, the former member for Lindsay who in 2018 announced her withdrawal from preselection at the following year's election after a hugely public complaints process involving former members of staff. I know nothing of what Ms Husar was like as a boss. Quite possibly, like lots of federal politicians, including some who have become prime minister, she was difficult and imperious, self-centred, demanding and shouty. I honestly do not know. But I do know that the offences of which this woman was accused include directing a male member of staff to do the dishes and asking staff to help with the three children of whom she is the sole parent. I would compare her experience with male custodial sole parents in the federal parliament, only I cannot think of a single one. My judgment may also be clouded by my acquaintance with many female political staffers who so routinely wash dishes, pick up dry cleaning, remember to organise clean socks for and – yes – look after the children of their male bosses that for them to complain about it would be thought completely crackers.

There is so much female work that only becomes questionable when done by a man. I refer you to the minor scandal of 2009 when eagle-eyed Liberal scandal-hunters noticed, on Prime Minister Kevin Rudd's flight manifest, an individual called John Fisher who was listed as "travelling assistant to the Prime Minister." Having an assistant or private secretary who takes care of protocol, packing and making sure your shoes are polished isn't that unusual for prime ministers. Usually these assistants are female and thought thoroughly unremarkable. But in Rudd's case it was a man, and the headline in The Daily Telegraph declared: "Meet Kevin Rudd's $78k 'party-boy' butler."

I'm sorry that I keep digressing into political examples. Parliament House is the workplace to which I've paid the most attention in the past two decades as a political reporter. And one of the things that continues to intrigue me is the way politics reflects us back to ourselves. The way expectations of how women and men who are public figures will behave is often a miniaturised, diamond-hard replica of the expectations we distribute more generally over a broader sample size.

And I very firmly believe that the underrepresentation of women in federal parliament is substantially due to women's knowledge that if they want to do what countless male politicians have done since Federation and have a family at the same time, they will be treated very differently. Which is why, historically, a disproportionate number of the women who have been very influential in Australian politics have either waited till their children were grown up first, or not had kids at all – Julia Gillard, Julie Bishop, Michaelia Cash, Amanda Vanstone and so on. (Of course, when they get there, helpful chaps like Bill Heffernan will accuse them of being "deliberately barren" and out of touch with the common experience, which must be nice for those women, for some of whom childlessness has literally been the price of admission to the place.) When Anna Burke – the Labor member for Chisholm – had a baby in 1999, she became only the second woman to give birth while serving in the House of Representatives.

But the good news is that this is changing. Just off the top of my head, I can think of twenty women who have had babies in parliament since then; some of them several babies. Nicola Roxon in 2007 became the first woman to serve in cabinet while raising a preschool-age child. The first! And in 2017, Kelly O'Dwyer became the first woman to give birth while serving as a cabinet minister. Increasingly, these female MPs have support-ive spouses who change the way they work to raise that kid. And that's useful, because a parliament that governs us should also reflect us.

If I am dwelling on this stuff, it's because I want to communicate the extraordinary, almost tectonic power of human assumptions, and the backlash when they are violated in some way. Deep down, we still broadly expect prime ministers to be men with helpful wives and grown-up children.

So, what – if anything – is changing in the world outside politics? We know already that the proportion of stay-at-home dads is low. But how do working dads arrange their time? Let's take a look at the overview, from the Australian Institute of Family Studies, using census data on families with at least one kid aged under twelve. More than 40 per cent of these mothers work part-time. But only 4 per cent of fathers work part-time. Forty-two per cent of mums work flexibly (this includes working part-time, working a compressed work week or flexible start and finish times, and working from home) compared to 30 per cent of dads. In fact, 60 per cent of dads report that they don't use any kind of flexibility in their work to deal with the demands of children and family. Sixty per cent! That's six in ten working Australian fathers who respond to parenthood by doing ... nothing different at all. And that's weird.

Australia's workplace laws do make provision for flexible work. Under section 65 of the *Fair Work Act* 2009, an employee who is a parent of a child school-age or younger, or a carer, or has a disability, or is aged over fifty-five, or is a victim of domestic violence has the right to request flexible work. The employer is obliged to consider the request in good faith. And the Fair Work Commission in September 2018 ruled that if an employer declines such a request, it must provide a reason.

But "flexism" – discrimination against workers who would like to work flexibly – is a term of increasing currency. And men who ask for flexible work are twice as likely to have their request refused as women, according to a 2016 study by business consulting group Bain and Company.

While workplaces commonly expect women to ask for flexible work, there's not the same degree of acceptance for men. In 2015, Craig and Cameron Zammit – twin brothers – ran into some difficulty with their long-term employer, the Liverpool Hospital in Sydney's south-western sub-urbs. Both worked there as painters. And for the previous eight years, both had started and finished work an hour early each day, working from 6 a.m. to 2.30 p.m., which enabled the men to collect their children from school at 3 p.m. But then the hospital's management decided to consolidate the work hours of employees. The Zammits were told that under a "whole of hospital" drive to improve response times and increase efficiency, they'd now be working from 7.00 a.m. until 3.30 p.m. The men and their union appealed to the NSW Industrial Relations Commission, arguing that women in the hospital's nursing and administrative divisions were encour-aged to work flexibly, but the same latitude was not granted to the all-male engineering area. An hour's difference would not affect health outcomes at the hospital, they argued, but would create significant inconvenience and expense for the low-paid Zammits, whose wives also worked and who would be obliged to employ a babysitter if their work-day ran until 3.30. The commission did not sympathise: the commissioner ruled that there was nothing unjust about the hours the men were being required to work. Also, he found that the hospital was within its rights to set the work hours of employees. And this is true: it was. But the hearing ran for four days. That's an expensive exercise. If two women in the administrative division of the hospital had wanted to start and finish an hour earlier, would the hospital have engaged in a similar legal fight to the death?

The history of regulated work–family balance in this country is not an especially long one. It's only fifty-four years ago, for instance, that the "Marriage Bar" – the legislative requirement that women working in the Commonwealth public service quit their jobs upon marriage – was finally lifted after a decade or so of nervous indecision within the Menzies government. Australia is still liberally populated with women who have a direct memory of being asked to quit their jobs when they got married. Or who – like my late mother-in-law, Jennifer Storer – were teachers and were forced to resign upon marriage and reapply for their jobs, losing all seniority and accrued leave and essentially starting again at the bottom. Women, it was felt, should resign from their jobs so as not to deprive a deserving man of the position, seeing as upon the acquisition of a husband and personal breadwinner they no longer had need of an income, and moreover would be required at home to supervise the forthcoming progeny. This policy had support from the male-dominated union movement at the time, which is one of the reasons it took so long to shake.

The election of the Whitlam government in 1972 changed things for many women. The 1972 Equal Pay Case raised women's salaries by around 30 per cent, and in June 1973 the Whitlam government passed the *Maternity Leave (Australian Government Employees) Act*. Around 64,000 women worked in the public service at the time, and the legislation entitled them to fifty-two weeks of maternity leave, twelve of which were to be on full pay. It also outlawed discrimination against employees on the grounds of pregnancy.

"Looking back over the history of paid parental leave, or paid maternity leave in Australia, it really was the public service that created the shift," recalls Jenny Macklin, who – nearly forty years after the *Maternity Leave Act* was legislated – created Australia's first general paid parental leave scheme. The pattern went like this: the Commonwealth started paying women maternity leave and granting unpaid leave for longer periods. Unions brought pressure to bear on large private-sector organisations to do the same, aided by the pressures of the competitive workplace. "If you go back to the Whitlam period, the introduction of paid parental leave in the public sector and the expansion over time ... the public sector has been really important," Macklin says. "And the private sector is important because it sets the norm. That's the way in which culture changes."

In the late 1990s, Macklin – a senior figure in the seemingly endless stretch of opposition that ensued for Labor after Paul Keating lost the 1996 election to John Howard's Coalition – began her internal campaign to install a universal public paid parental leave scheme in her party's policy platform. Her allies were powerful union women Jennie George and Sharan Burrow, who both served terms as president of the ACTU. "I had plenty of old fogey blokes in the union movement who thought women should be at home," Macklin recalls. "Getting it into the Labor platform was a real effort. Sharan and Jennie were instrumental."

When Labor finally made it into government in 2007, the global financial crisis hit soon after, crimping the ambitions of ministers like Macklin in spending portfolios – in her case, family and community services. But Macklin was a powerful – if publicly unassuming – minister in the Rudd and Gillard governments. Her policy legacy from a straitened period in public administration (not to mention one of vicious internal political tensions) is impressive, paid parental leave and the National Disability Insurance Scheme being the most notable. "Our goal was to get something legislated," says Macklin of the parental leave scheme. "That was really fundamental for me. To break this drought in Australia, which had us as one of only two developed countries in the world without a public scheme." During her internal battle to promote paid parental leave as a public scheme, Macklin also had strong allies in the private sector – women like Heather Ridout, of the Australian Institute of Company Directors, and Ann Sherry, who was then at Westpac. "Having those people, working in the private sector – we wouldn't have got where we got, and I wouldn't have been able to do what I did, if they hadn't prepared the ground."

Designing the scheme in government required close attention to existing Australian values, Macklin argues. For her, this ruled out a European-style public scheme in which taxpayers fund the full replacement wage of the parental leave recipient.

> There had to be this cultural shift towards paid leave – that was the first thing. But we also, in Australia, have a very highly targeted social security system. So the notion of going to a European full-pay approach I did not think was ever going to happen.
>
> The Productivity Commission inquiry recommended it be set at the minimum wage. I thought that did reflect the Australian view – that taxpayers should pay basic support but not the full replacement wage. That was part of my reasoning for also introducing a means test, which doesn't exist in Europe.

And so, on 17 June 2010, the Australian parliament legislated the nation's first paid parental leave scheme. Australia was, as Macklin says, the second-last Western country without one; the United States now sails on alone in this respect. "Given the global financial crisis, it was an absolute miracle that we got it through at all," says Macklin. "There were a few resisters ... but that's a story for another time when a few people are dead." Laughing, she adds: "Quite a few people."

The Opposition was led, at the time, by Tony Abbott, whose attitude to paid parental leave was defined by his Howard-era promise that it would happen "over this government's dead body," right up until the point at which he executed a lithe reversal and announced that an Abbott government would include a "gold-plated" maternity leave scheme in which women would be paid not just the minimum wage but a replacement wage of their actual salaries, funded by the public purse. Abbott announced the policy without first gaining the approval of his shadow cabinet. The captain, he claimed, was entitled to make a few calls in a political party, and as he sunnily observed, "It's better to ask forgiveness than to seek permission." Many were surprised by the reversal in Abbott's views. But when questioned later about it, Abbott's wife, Margie, explained the reason in one word: "Daughters." The couple had three daughters in their late teens and entering the workforce when Abbott had his epiphany.

If I may digress for a moment (and I justify this on the grounds that the digression does pursue one of the purposes of this essay, which is to explore ways in which attitudes and human customs can be changed): daughters are a force of their own. Having daughters makes male executives more generous to their female employees, according to a 2012 study, *Fatherhood and Managerial Style*. And where politicians are concerned, the effects of daughters are readily identifiable. The Yale economist Ebonya Washington, in a 2008 study, found a distinct gap between the way male and female members of Congress voted on women's issues, but every daughter born to a male congressman closed that gap, on average, by one-quarter. That is to say, men changed their minds on women's issues more and more with each daughter they fathered. Interesting, huh? Anyway, back to the narrative.

The Coalition eventually voted in support of Macklin's policy, but reserved the right to improve the paid parental leave scheme in government. Abbott's colleagues backed his "gold-plated" version in public, but moaned bitterly in private about its expense, and the fact that Abbott planned to fund it with a levy on big business. During this period, journalists extracted hours of fun from asking Abbott's colleagues in interviews how they felt about the policy. Watching them defend – through gritted fangs – a policy they so thoroughly loathed was a base form of entertainment but a satisfying one nonetheless.

"People couldn't believe it," says Macklin. "I knew it was never going to get through. The Australian people were never going to accept the idea that the taxpayer would pay someone everything that they earn. That's fine for the employer to do; they get the benefit. But we've never had that European social insurance approach. I just didn't think it was going to fly."

Abbott's Liberal colleagues didn't like the impost on big business, and the party arranged for a compensatory cut to the corporate tax rate. More broadly, suspicion about the scheme's design feature of paying more to higher-paid recipients ran deep in a country accustomed to means-testing and a progressive approach to taxation.

At the third and final leaders' debate between Tony Abbott and Kevin Rudd – held at Rooty Hill during the concluding stages of the 2013 election – delivery driver Ian Barker, of Seven Hills, delivered a memorable critique of the Abbott policy. "I give the commonsense test to policies," he began. "Now your policy of paid parental leave is a great policy, but I just think the forklift driver in Mount Druitt shouldn't be paying his taxes so a pretty little lady lawyer on the North Shore earning 180,000 a year can have a kid."

Mr Barker put it more bluntly than most, of course, but the thread of resentment is important to understanding deep public feeling about paid parental leave: that in some ways, it's seen as money for jam.

It was a curious position for Australian working parents. No paid parental scheme for more than a century, and then suddenly two turn up at once. Macklin's policy was modest; eighteen weeks at the minimum wage for the "primary carer." "We called the first one Paid Parental Leave on purpose," she explains. "After the first six weeks it can go to either partner. That was a design feature. We did feel very strongly that the first part should belong to the mother, because recovering from birth is a real thing." The scheme had a secondary measure: "Dad and Partner Pay," which consisted of two weeks, also at the minimum wage. "The reason we did Dad and Partner Pay was [because] we also knew that it's very important for dads to bond with their newborn babies ... to have time together at the beginning ... to meet this new little person and frankly just to cope." Calling the secondary scheme "Dad and Partner Pay" ("partner" was to cover same-sex parents, Macklin says) also did something else. It made it very clear who was expected to be the primary carer, and who the secondary.

And parents followed suit. We've had a federal paid parental leave in Australia for nine years now. In that time, more than a million women have claimed the principal government paid parental leave scheme. To be precise: 1,236,675, on the latest figures from the Department of Social Services. In that time, 6250 men have taken primary carer leave under the scheme. That puts the rate of men's involvement at 0.5 per cent. Half of one per cent of the number of mothers. Claimants of the Dad and Partner Pay scheme, which has been in place since 2013, stand at 485,044 men and just 2094 women. Less than half of one per cent of those claiming secondary caregiver leave are women, in other words. But also, intriguingly, for every ten women claiming primary parental leave, there are only four men claiming Dad and Partner Pay. Even allowing for the happy capacity of same-sex couples to claim – as they are fully entitled and indeed encouraged to do – that is a lot of chaps who are either running serious polygamy rackets or who aren't taking any parental leave at all.

In the world of employer-funded leave, the split is a tiny bit less discouraging. Of the private-sector employees who take primary carer leave, one in twenty is a man. But obviously, it's still quite the gap. And it makes me think about the private-sector employers who offer generous parental leave schemes. The ones who are doing the right thing and looking after their employees who need to take time out to have a child. Of which claimants 95 per cent are women. Doesn't that mean that, effectively, a responsible employer with a female-dominated workforce is effectively cross-subsidising the employers of her employees' husbands? I remember the moment when I was approached after a speech by an employer of many women who quietly made this point. I felt stupid for never having joined those dots before, but of course she's right. It's just so unremarkable as a human pattern of behaviour that we never really think about it as a serious structural kink in the workforce.

And a lot of people will say: well, of course it's the mum who's taking the leave. She's the one with the boobs, she's the one who's spent nine months using only her abdomen to make a whole person and then be responsible for getting it the hell out of there. I get it. And in no way would

I ever argue that men and women are identical, or even that they necessarily respond to parenthood in the same way. But in my view, the wants and needs and proclivities can vary so wildly from human to human, in just about every respect, that it seems foolish to pretend that physical hardware should predetermine too much. (If you get into a backyard barbecue argument about this and someone tries to tell you that men's and women's brains are different, then make sure you've read Angela Saini's stunning and compellingly readable 2018 book *Inferior*; it will give you all the ammunition you need.)

What worries me is that in Australia the taking of parental leave tends to be an either/or thing. In a heterosexual couple, it's either Mum or Dad. And that's usually going to be primary carer leave for Mum, and two weeks at best for Dad, who – if my personal experience is any guide – will generally use that time shuttling to and from the chemist, and trying unsuccessfully to assemble a flat-pack shed. (Always with the shed. Maybe it's just us.) In this country, we know pretty much who's supposed to take parental leave and who probably won't. And there are all sorts of knock-on effects from these assumptions. The person who takes the parental leave invariably becomes the person who knows more about nappy-changing, more about which food the kid likes, more about nap times and play dates and which kids at the park have nut allergies. All the stuff that is part of the grand ephemera of early parenthood. But that parent is also the person most likely to go back to work part-time. Also, the person most likely to take a job that isn't exactly the one they're trained for or that isn't the best paid, but the flexibility is good so it'll do. That person is also the person most likely to say, "Well, my salary doesn't even cover child care, so I'm just going to take a break for now." That person, when the next baby comes along, is absolutely the person who's going to be the primary carer, because this time it's a no-brainer. And then one thing leads to another and suddenly everyone's at retirement age, at which point an Australian woman will on average have a superannuation balance that's 42 per cent less than that of an average Australian man.

You see how these patterns establish themselves?

When people have babies, they are embarking on a new and terrifying phase of life. Who knows how to work a baby? Hardly anyone, contrary to certain generalised beliefs that women in particular are born with a special knack for this stuff. Essentially, you have to *learn* how to look after a baby, and it is strange and scary. You are coming to terms with the fact that you are now a hostage to fortune. Your dreams are full of unthinkable terrors concerning what might happen to the baby. In your waking moments, you dully register that this fleet of new worries isn't going anywhere; fear of cot death will give way to fear of choking, drowning or swallowing the tiny button batteries you only just found out are lethal, and thence to abduction, bullying, then drugs, car accidents and so on. Those waking moments are plenteous, because you're not getting any sleep.

To summarise: parents of babies are tired and scared pretty much all of the time. So of all the times in your life when you're going to look around you and just do whatever everyone else seems to be doing – this is the peak moment for that kind of decision-making. All the other dads at work took two weeks off, so that's what we'll do. All the other mums took a year off, so we'll do that too.

And that's how national patterns work.

"I think there are two reasons men don't take parental leave," says Jenny Macklin. "One is money. The other is culture. Money is still a huge problem because men earn more than women. I think the capacity for families to manage even with the paid parental leave that we introduced is already stretched – the women go off on four months on the minimum wage, which is less than a lot of them are earning. [Families will] take a wage drop, but they're just not prepared to do it on the man's income."

On the matter of culture, Sex Discrimination Commissioner Kate Jenkins says of men: "When they have children, that's often their first experience of discrimination. They see the gendered rules, and how it can work against you, where mostly the discrimination works in their favour."

The Abbott scheme never saw the light of legislative day. The Coalition was elected within weeks of Mr Barker's critique at Rooty Hill, but the parental leave scheme was lost in early 2015. Mr Abbott jettisoned it in a desperate attempt to repair his internal stocks, just days after he horrified colleagues by knighting Prince Philip in the Australia Day honours list. And in the May Budget a few months later, treasurer Joe Hockey unveiled a new tack: the government would legislate to prevent parents "double-dipping" – taking the public package on top of anything their employers paid by way of entitlements. "What I'm saying to you is I think it is unfair that someone can be receiving from the taxpayers a paid parental leave scheme, such as an employee of the government, and then they can go to Centrelink and get another paid parental leave scheme paid for by tax-payers," Mr Hockey told the ABC's 7.30 that night. "We think that double-dipping is unfair. Of course you get a minimum of $11,500 and that's guaranteed if your employer does not give you that money. But if they do, then it's meant to be a safety net, it's not a salary topper."

Scott Morrison, then minister for social services, described the practice as "a rort." This interpretation was at odds with the explicit wording of the *Paid Parental Leave Act 2010*, which specified that, "The financial support provided by this Act is intended to complement and supplement existing entitlements to paid or unpaid leave in connection with the birth or adoption of a child." But for a government that had failed to legislate a significant chunk of the cuts it had sensationally announced a year earlier in the controversial 2014 Budget, this tweak to the paid parental leave scheme was a profitable idea: cutting benefits to around 88,000 parents would deliver $1 billion in savings.

The curse of paid parental leave, however, had not quite finished with Tony Abbott. Within days of the Budget, it emerged that both the finance minister, Mathias Cormann, and the assistant treasurer, Josh Frydenberg, had themselves benefited from doubling up on private and public schemes upon the births of their children. This news occasioned a further strategic huddle, and the new line thereafter was that it was perfectly okay for women to exercise their legal entitlements as they stood, but the government remained of the view that in future they should be entitled to either one form of leave or the other, but not both.

As is probably unsurprising given this rather meandering course of events, the policy itself died a quiet and unlamented death in late 2015. Malcolm Turnbull challenged successfully for the leadership in September and the changes to the paid parental leave scheme were among the Abbott-era policies with which the new prime minister did not persist. It's worth recalling these events, however, if for no other reason than to register the tone of the debate. Parental leave payments are for "pretty little lady lawyers" and "rorters." The suggestion is unmistakeable: receiving public money to care for a baby is at some level a bit of a scam – money for nothing.

Anyone who's ever done it for any length of time knows, of course, that caring for an infant can involve a degree of exhaustion distinctly more bone-crunching than any incurred in the execution of paid work. But the people who have done this work are habitually underrepresented among the ranks of those who make decisions about paid parental leave. And if caring for a child is such lowly work that devoting public money to it raises eyebrows – well, it's hardly surprising that men as a class don't feel madly tempted to get involved.

Right. So we've established that men don't – in the main – take parental leave beyond the two-week cigar break that the Australian culture views as permissible. We know that men are slightly more likely than they were to work flexibly, but nowhere near as likely as women, and that hardly any of them go so far as to work part-time. This is true even for workplaces with flexible work policies that are officially available to both genders. Somehow, the men know on some molecular level that these policies and entitlements are not really meant for them.

As I said earlier, there isn't an awful lot of research in Australia into why this is so, or where the wellspring is for these forces so extraordinarily powerful that they can shape the behaviour of millions of people without ever being codified, and indeed do so even where formal rules explicitly direct the opposite. But a survey in 2017 conducted by recruitment agency Hays gives a good indication of where the sticking points are. The firm asked 842 men and women about access to parental leave, and only 19 per cent of respondents believed that their employers treated men and women equally in this respect. Of the men surveyed, 54 per cent said they were reluctant to take leave because to do so would damage their families finan-cially. And 34 per cent said they feared they'd be seen as less committed at work. Twelve per cent of respondents said that parental leave was the right and responsibility of the mother.

In 2015, at the University of Adelaide, researchers Ashlee Borgkvist, Vivienne Moore, Jaklin Elliott and Shona Crabb (no relation!) decided to talk to some fathers in great depth about the decisions they made at work and why. It was a small group – fifteen men, carefully chosen and inter-viewed separately at substantial length. Not just about the decisions they made as fathers, but also about what they felt were the expectations of them. Many of these men worked full-time, and many employed some kind of flexibility. Gary, for example, a 33-year-old acquisitions manager, was taking an hour off in the mornings to read with his daughter at school.

Ernie, a 52-year-old social planner, had used accrued time to go on school visits with his wife and daughter. But he'd not gone to the most recent visit, for fear of pushing his luck. What was fascinating about the men's accounts was that, commonly, their caution about undertaking these activities was not due to explicit workplace rules prohibiting flexible work; it was about their own desire to be seen as a good worker, and not someone who slacked off. Most of the men were doing more caring work than is average for Australian men, but they saw themselves as exceptions, outliers; in many cases they saw their flexible work as a privilege, or a function of their seniority or their good standing with the boss. Something that they got away with, in other words. Not something to which they were generally entitled. Nick, a 42-year-old team leader, had recently asked his boss for a day off: "Because we have a strong relationship and I do a lot of, um, work that makes his life easier ... he will accommodate back ... so that's how all those relationships work – if you don't have that, it won't work."

Significantly, the men tended to describe and identify themselves with reference to their work and their need to provide for their families, not through their roles as carers. They explained their flexible work as something they'd *earned* through being good workers; it was all calculated by reference to work. In Nick's case, that work identity was so valuable that it superseded even the most prosaic hip-pocket calculation. "In reality, if [my wife] worked full-time and I worked part-time, the income would probably end up being more, but I've worked my way to where I am for a long time ... so it would be absolutely silly to stop now and go part-time," he said.

This comment stuck with me. The argument for mothers not returning to work, or returning to work part-time, is usually framed as a financial one: "He earns more, so it would make no sense for him to go part-time or stay at home. And my wage would barely cover child care," and so on. This argument often misses the long-term ramifications for women of staying out of work for protracted periods: increased vulnerability in the event of a break-up or bereavement, for instance, loss of promotions and pay rises, and a permanently depressed superannuation account. But Nick is powered by more than money; he's saying that even to behave in a financially rational way and arrange the family's work commitments to maximise income would be "silly" because it would strip him of his significance and his life's work.

I remember speaking at an industry dinner several years ago, just after *The Wife Drought* was published. The dinner was full of superannuation executives, whom I harangued good-naturedly for twenty minutes or so about the expectations that commonly accompanied women to work. After the dinner, I found myself in conversation with a man — he must have been in his mid-thirties, I think — who told me that he and his wife were shortly expecting their second child. "Personally, I would absolutely love to take extended parental leave," he told me. "It's just that in my job I'm not really replaceable."

"And what would happen if you were female?" I asked him.

From his furrowed brow, it was apparent that he had not considered this question before. This question — *how will I hold on to my identity and my role at work, while also managing my child (or sick relative, or any other domestic obligation)?* — is one with whose curves, knots and grooves many working women are exhaustedly familiar. The fact that you can still find a man to whom it has genuinely never occurred is a demonstration of the enduring strength of the "ideal employee" model.

The men in the Borgkvist study talk of eking out small privileges in the flexible work stakes: an hour off to attend a school event, a good relationship with a boss who doesn't mind if they take a day here or there. The men are constrained most powerfully by their own need to be a good worker, to fulfil the expectation that they will work hard. And yet the idea that women will work part-time is entirely unremarkable, and not accompanied by the same agonising calculus. Gary, for instance, when asked if anybody else works flexibly, says: "They happen all, I think, to be females, and a number of them work part-time, so we've got an accountant who works in between school hours so she's got the time to drop off the kids and pick them up."

This is the heart of the matter, surely? We know and have accepted that women can go to university and join the army and work down mines and so on. We know and have accepted that a woman's capacity in a job is the same as a man's; this concept is no longer radical. So how can it be that working a compressed work week, working part-time or taking parental leave for a chunk of time is deeply unremarkable – indeed, expected – for women, and yet for men it's a matter of privilege, luck or indeed in some cases flatly unthinkable? It's the same job. The same equation. The same rearrangement of matter when a woman takes six months off from Job X as when a man does. But the neural tissue we've built around these ideas makes those circumstances unrecognisable, one from the other.

If my new friend from the superannuation dinner were a woman, the world wouldn't end. She'd take parental leave and someone would step up and fill in for a few months or even a year, and then she'd come back and the company would not only have her back, but would also have gained someone who'd accumulated new experience and expertise. I mean, it's not easy, exactly, but it's also really not that hard. Somehow we've constructed a system of expectations, though, in which a man who is doing his job is bound to it by something much deeper and more fibrous than his contract of employment, or even his need to provide. Stopping work for a while, or even just doing less of it, is thus not as simple as a law telling him it's allowed. It involves finding and loosening restraints far more ancient than those outlined in any human resources manual; knots which have swelled with age and seawater; ropes that have bitten into the skin. But they need to come off. Why should they bind only men?

Much is written about work–family stress among working mothers. But fathers suffer too. A brand-new study from the Australian Institute of Family Studies – published in June 2019 – looked at about 3500 dads drawn from their Longitudinal Study of Australian Children, conducted in partnership with the government and the Australian Bureau of Statistics. This study has been underway since 2003, and tracks 10,000 children who were babies at the time it commenced and are now in their teens.

Researcher Amanda Cooklin examined the experience of 3460 fathers in the study, and established a clear link between long work hours, high work–family conflict and poor mental health. This was true across skilled and semi-skilled workers, and men of all income groups. "When fathers moved into high work–family conflict, from one wave to the next, their mental health also deteriorated," she concluded. "When fathers 'escaped' out of high work–family conflict (i.e. from high work–family conflict in one wave to low/no conflict in the next) their mental health also showed significant improvement." The key factors for high work–family conflict and resultant psychological distress? They include: long work hours, lack of flexibility, and not having access to paid family-related leave.

*

Our expectations of fathers are changing. Absenteeism isn't accepted the way it once was. Gone are the days when fathers were considered some-how an optional extra to the parenting process, like rear spoilers or metallic duco. And yet there's something stuck for dads. Something is standing in the way of them responding to those demands by being around more.

Recent research by the Diversity Council of Australia – conducted among young fathers – gives us a glimpse of the significant gap between what the new generation of dads would like to do and what they actually do. Of these fathers (aged thirty-five years and younger), 79 per cent wanted the flexibility to choose their start and finish times at work. But only 41 per cent of them actually did so. Similarly, 79 per cent of them wanted to work a compressed working week. But only 24 per cent of them actually did that. And while 56 per cent of these young fathers wanted to be able to work at least some of their hours at home, it was only actually happening for 13 per cent of them.

Okay. So what's stopping these men? Australian research in this area is still frustratingly sketchy. But we know from the major survey of around

1000 Australian businesspeople undertaken by Bain that men were about twice as likely as women to have their requests for flexible work refused. And the same study confirmed that men's experience with flexible work and parental leave was very different from women's. Fascinatingly, women who worked flexibly were more confident and ambitious within their companies, as well as much more likely to endorse their companies and recommend them as a workplace. But among men, the reverse was true. Men who worked flexibly were significantly less confident of promotion than men who didn't. And they were much less likely to endorse their own companies than those who worked routine hours. Male respondents reported they'd been told that flexible working was more of a woman's thing. Also that there was no way they'd be promoted if they worked part-time.

Now, no one is suggesting that what every dad really wants to do is get home from work at 4 p.m. every day so as to be sure to catch that excellent juncture where the juvenile and the adult stores of patience expire within fifteen minutes of each other. When I first read Edith Gray's research indicating that the average Australian father worked five hours more a week after the birth of his first child, somewhere deep down inside I grinned in recognition and thought: you sly dogs. There is something about the workplace, with its principles of reward for effort, with its adult company and relatively clean workspaces, that can seem more appealing than the unrecompensed crapshoot that is raising a small child.

What role does male ambivalence play in this pattern of behaviour? How many fathers are secretly relieved to be free of the dinner/bath/bed shift and glad of the protection afforded by workplace norms obliging them to stay at work till it's over? I don't know; no one does. There may be plenty of women who feel the same way. But research indicates that the more involvement a father has early in his child's life, the deeper and more fulfilling his relationship with that child will be. So no matter what proportion of fathers it is who genuinely would like to deepen their relationships with their children, isn't it worth allowing them to do so?

And if we're serious about women's participation in the workplace – and given the double shift worked by the majority of working mothers in this country, that can only feasibly be achieved by giving them a hand at home – then that means being serious about men having the opportunity to leave it, when they need to, just like women do. Changing the way you work when your life changes is a normal, rational, sensible thing to do. But somehow we're stuck on the idea that it's a normal, rational, *lady* thing to do.

I'll give you an example which – while tiny – has stuck in my mind for years now. After *The Wife Drought* was published, I heard from lots of readers. Lots of men, actually, which encouraged me in my belief that men, too, are chafing at the straitjacket of gendered expectations at work.

Hands down the best correspondence I had after publication, if I may digress for a moment, was from a guy whose wife was going back to work after the birth of their first child. Both of them were worried because the kid was still breastfeeding and refusing to take a bottle. Now, this was exactly the same problem I had had with my third child, Kate. At three months of age, she accompanied me on a tour of Australia shooting a series of *Kitchen Cabinet*, during which Kate would be strapped to the chest of the series' producer, Madeleine, while I was on camera, and Madeleine would walk up and down outside Malcolm Turnbull's place, or wherever, with a remote earpiece in her ear listening to the interview taking place, and when Kate woke up the two of them would come in for a break and a feed. The bottle refusal made things tricky later on with Kate, but I discovered that she would cheerily take food off a spoon. So, after a midnight epiphany, I went through a short, weird but totally practical phase of making jellied breastmilk. I put this in the book, then took it out because it was gross, then put it back in because it was true, then agonised, then thought, bugger it. Let it stay. And so a guy on Twitter with the bottle problem got in touch with me to ask for instructions on how to make jellied breastmilk. I've got to say, I've had some weird exchanges on social media over the years, but this was in my Top One. And the day he messaged me to say his wife had had her first day back at work and the kid was mad for the fancy panna cotta, I felt so proud it was like I'd raised the kid myself. The thing I loved about this guy was that he didn't view the feeding issue as his wife's problem. He viewed it as a family problem, and one that they solved together.

But back to the little exchange that haunts me. I heard from a young woman who was approaching the birth of her first baby. Both she and her husband were teachers. She wrote: "Both of us requested a discussion about returning to work part-time after the birth. My school: Sure! How many days do you want to work? His school: Sorry. Not an option." And for me, that kind of sums it up.

It's exactly the response Anna Burke's husband had when Anna, having won the seat of Chisholm in the 1998 election and got pregnant – two amazing life events – realised just how unaccustomed Parliament House was to having a newborn around. Her husband, a Victorian paramedic, applied for parental leave so that he could go to Canberra with Anna and the baby. Not an option, he was told. In the end, after he persevered, and brought in his union, and cracked out the Macquarie Dictionary to demonstrate that he fulfilled the formal definition of "parent," he got his leave. But what worries me is that lots of men don't ask. Don't persevere. Or succumb to the – I have to say, well-founded – fear that they will be penalised at work for asking.

Working flexibly or part-time is something it is assumed mothers will probably do; no one is surprised when they ask for it. And for all the things women are rubbish at asking for in workplaces (more money, more responsibility, promotions, more recognition for the work they're doing), the thing they're really excellent at asking for is flexibility.

In May 2017, Derek Rotondo sent an email to HR. He and his wife were awaiting the birth of their second child, and Rotondo was requesting parental leave for the arrival. Rotondo – a fraud investigator with the American investment bank JPMorgan Chase – had taken just two weeks of leave for the birth of his first son, and wished he could have taken more. So when his employer, in 2016, announced it was increasing the amount of paid parental leave for primary caregivers from twelve to sixteen weeks, Rotondo pricked up his ears.

The firm's policy was much more generous than that provided by most employers in the United States, which as we have seen is the only Western nation not to have some form of public paid parental leave. But Rotondo was surprised to receive notification that his request had been denied. "Per our policy, birth mothers are what we consider as the primary caregivers," the email explained. Essentially, JPMorgan Chase would not allow Rotondo to take primary carer's leave unless he could prove to them that his wife – a school teacher – was being forced to return to work, or was physically or mentally unwell to a degree that she was unable to care for their child. He was entitled to two weeks' leave.

"Like we all do, I started googling ... I thought, 'This doesn't sound right,'" he later told NBC's *Today Show*. Rotondo called a workplace law centre and was eventually directed to the American Council of Civil Liberties, which helped him to commence legal action. JPMorgan Chase capitulated as soon as he issued proceedings, approving the full period of leave. But he kept the legal action going in order to establish a formal precedent, and in May 2019 the bank announced that it would retrain its human resources staff to ensure the leave policy was offered without discrimination. It also established a $5 million fund to compensate fathers short-changed in the past.

"I wasn't going to be one of those dads who was constantly working, missing the first home run, first touchdown, any of those moments,"

Rotondo explained. When his first son was born, he had gone straight back to work and Rotondo's wife was the parent who learned how to settle the baby, and became expert in all the myriad details of infant care. But when the bank finally agreed to let him take four months of parental leave with his second son, Lincoln, Rotondo discovered he was actually very good at getting babies to sleep. He was able to ease his wife's fatigue by taking over at night, free from anxiety about having to go to work tired. "I'm a baby whisperer!" he told the Huffington Post.

Derek Rotondo is not the only American plaintiff to challenge the assumption that parental leave policies are intended for female employees only. In August 2018, the cosmetics giant Estée Lauder settled a class action brought by male employees who claimed they were denied the parental leave entitlements available to their female colleagues. And in 2015, broadcaster CNN settled a case brought by former correspondent Josh Levs. Levs' third child was born prematurely in 2013. He had already asked for parental leave, which the broadcaster offered at the rate of ten weeks at full pay for biological mothers, or parents of either gender who adopted or had a child through a surrogate. "My employer, Time Warner, had an extremely unusual policy," Levs later told The Washington Post. "Anyone could get ten weeks of paid leave to take care of a new child – except the man who'd impregnated the mother of his child. Me. The biological father. I went to Time Warner, privately, quietly … I said, 'I'm needed at home when my baby will be born in a few months.' They didn't give me an answer for months. Then my daughter was born early and I was holding my tiny, preemie daughter in my arms, going back and forth, asking for an answer. They finally said no." Levs went on to write a best-selling book about male culture and parenting, and his employer settled his case, and improved its parental leave offering for fathers to six weeks.

Levs said he felt like he'd "opened the floodgates," such was the response from men he received when he initiated the case. "They want to be home more, yet they're under pressure to be providers. That work–life conflict is leading to stress, that can mess with your mental health, and mess with your physical life. All this stuff is intertwined. When your life is forced to be this frenetic, because we have policies that don't make sense, we're hurting business, we're hurting men, we're hurting women ... and we're hurting children." The former parental leave policy at his work, he says, was calculated to stop men from taking leave, but the ramifications were in fact much broader: "As long as you're pushing men to stay at work, you're pushing women to stay home."

In 2010, lawyer Ariel Ayanna issued legal proceedings against his former employer, the law firm Dechert. Ayanna testified that he had been a high-achieving and valued member of the firm's Boston office before his wife – upon the birth of the couple's second child – developed an acute mental illness, requiring Ayanna to take leave to care for her through the birth of the child and thereafter. Ayanna took leave legally available to him but claimed that on his return he was severely punished. Colleagues criticised his absence, and the firm withheld work from him, citing his tendency to let his family life interfere with his work. Ultimately, he was fired in 2008 on the grounds that he had failed to meet his required billable hours. "The culture for men at Dechert is a 'macho' one which praises and encourages male associates and partners to fulfil the stereotypical male role of ceding family responsibilities to women," Ayanna argued in his statement of claim. "In this culture, caregiving is for wives of male attorneys and tolerated only for female attorneys. The firm culture does not require female attorneys to conform to the 'macho' stereotype." In the end, the firm settled the claim on undisclosed terms.

The language of "primary carers" is omnipresent in workplace policies and legislation. As Jenny Macklin explained, the language was adopted to allow for same-sex parents. But over the years, "primary carer" has become code for "birth mother" – this is an assumption that applies even where the parents are two women. In Australia, the public scheme is available to birth mothers, who then need to transfer the leave if they want their partner to take it. And as the above litigants in the United States have found out, the seeming gender neutrality of the language masks a very powerful set of assumptions about who we expect in practice to be that primary carer.

Australia may have the edge on the United States in terms of paid parental leave, but we have all the same historical assumptions about whose job it really is to raise children and keep house. So when I read about the Rotondo case and the legal phenomenon of fathers claiming a better deal from discriminatory parental leave entitlements in the States, my first thought was to look for comparable cases in Australia.

Here, the first port of call for discrimination complaints is the Equal Opportunity Commission. So I called Kate Jenkins, the Sex Discrimination Commissioner, a Melbourne-based lawyer who has a blended family of five children and a long history of working with male-dominated enterprises (the Australian Defence Force, the AFL). I wanted to know if there were many cases in Australia of men taking legal action against their workplaces for refusing them parental leave or flexible work. And it turns out that the answer is: no. There aren't many cases. Because in Australia, the *Sex Discrimination Act* explicitly allows employers to discriminate against men when making decisions about parental leave. Here's the section:

> Section 31: Pregnancy, childbirth or breastfeeding.
>
> Nothing in Division 1 or 2 renders it unlawful for a person to discriminate against a man on the ground of his sex by reason only of the fact that the firstmentioned person grants to a woman rights or privileges in connection with pregnancy, childbirth or breastfeeding.

Jenkins said the Commission is well aware that men face discrimination around their roles as fathers. In 2014, its landmark report on pregnancy and parental leave established that 27 per cent of fathers who took some kind of leave around the birth of a child reported harassment or discrimination on their return, ranging from negative comments to threats of dismissal. Jenkins said, "They only ask for two weeks leave max, but

I talk to a lot of men who say that in their workplaces, even that's not acceptable."

Jenkins did have one solitary Australian case study to which she could direct me. In 2017, the Australian Federal Police sought approval from the Fair Work Commission for a new enterprise agreement with its staff. One of the new terms in the agreement was a further four weeks of maternity leave for birth mothers, additional to the twelve weeks already contained in the *Maternity Leave (Commonwealth Employees) Act 1973*, legislated by the Whitlam government. Christopher Budd, an AFP employee and staff bargaining representative, challenged the new clause on the basis that it was sexist. He argued that fathers too should have access to the full suite of leave entitlements, and the fact that they were entitled to a lesser amount was based on a discriminatory notion that a man could not be a primary carer. But the Fair Work Commission rejected his arguments, partly because the *Sex Discrimination Act* explicitly permits employers to treat mothers and fathers differently. Budd appealed to the Commission's full bench, but lost. The case received desultory coverage.

How fascinating it is – ironic, too – that employers who discriminate against fathers are expressly permitted to do so by the nation's landmark anti-discrimination legislation. It's a cogent lesson in unintended consequences. When the *Sex Discrimination Act* was legislated by the Hawke government in 1984, its main aim was to make workplaces safer and fairer for women, who were then moving into the workforce in great numbers and encountering harassment and discrimination. Section 31 was there as a safeguard, ensuring that maternity leave could not be seen as an instance of gender discrimination. At the time, the idea that a man would be the primary carer was an exotic one indeed.

Jenkins says she's thought a lot of late about how the history and evolution of paid parental leave in Australia has contributed to modern attitudes. The introduction in the 1970s of one year's total paid and unpaid leave for women in the public service was, she says, pivotal. "That came about because we had good unions. We had to fight for that," she recalls. "But one of the perverse outcomes, when you jump to today, is that that hard-fought industrial gain actually locked in assumptions about who should stay home in the first twelve months, and whose salary was not so important." Now, says Jenkins, women tend to assume that one year is the right amount of time for them to be away from work. But a year is a long time. During that year, she says, women often assume the lion's share of childcare, cleaning and cooking, and at the end of the year they're unable to countenance the idea of combining the existing heavy workload with going back to paid work. The ideal length of time for parental leave is quite a complex and delicate equation. Twelve months is the norm, she has learned, but sometimes it's too long. "When women say they're pregnant, I don't want to be hard on them but when women tell me, oh, I'm having twelve months, I always ask — are you sure? Have you done your research?"

The days of "maternity leave" are largely behind us. Policies today talk about "primary carers" and "secondary carers." Yet, as we have seen, primary carer pretty much means the mum, most of the time, and the above-discussed litigation in the United States commonly arises when this cosy assumption is breached.

The broader — bolder — question is: why do we assume that when there are two parents, one needs to be the primary, and one the secondary, carer? Emma Walsh, the CEO of advocacy group Parents At Work, spends much of her time challenging this assumption. "We've got to get rid of this idea of primary and secondary carers, because no parent defines themselves like that," she says. That means letting each family decide. Everyone has different circumstances, everyone works differently, some may have post-natal depression to deal with, and so on. The most successful countries at managing work and family, Walsh says, do so from a position of absolute equality: the idea that fathers are just as important as mothers.

> But that's not how we approach it in Australia — here, it's a system designed for mothers. Fathers are an afterthought. So we don't have gender equality around parental leave. Men have been excluded —

and that needs to shift. It's now time to do this. Pretty much every other policy has been balanced for gender equality. They've gone through them all, they've harmonised all of them.

The last bastion – the last one that hasn't really been touched – is the parental leave policies. The research tells us that if we do, it's not just about the immediate uplift in women's capacity to go back to work faster. The uplift has been in child care, saving child care costs, [and] also at the other end of the spectrum in emotional bonding between fathers and their children.

There are so many taboos around parental leave. Men taking it is one of them. Another is the even more shocking concept of both parents taking extended leave at the same time. "I think we have to change the language so that we equalise it," says Walsh. "That does mean coming to terms with the fact that there will be some parents off at the same time. And that's okay. We all agree that annual leave is okay. We don't say, 'But you can't both have it at the same time.'"

As an advocate, Walsh's primary work is to encourage organisations to think laterally, and to challenge their own assumptions about how men and women will behave. The first reservation, of course, is cost. Extended periods of parental leave mean chunks of time for which an employer is paying a worker not to work. A hard sell. But less so when you consider the economic benefits of holding on to a good employee in whom you've invested training resources. For instance, when Google extended its parental leave offering from twelve weeks' paid leave to eighteen weeks, the rate of female turnover after maternity leave halved. Attracting and retaining talent is a significant issue for many modern organisations, and parental leave entitlements can be a valuable incentive: a 2016 survey by Deloitte found that 77 per cent of employees said the paid parental leave influenced their choice of employer. For global organisations like Spotify, the results speak for themselves. When it launched its world-leading parental leave equality policy in 2015, which offered seven months' paid leave to men and women, its ability to attract talent skyrocketed. It now boasts that thousands of people apply to work for it every month. Perhaps surprisingly, Spotify reports that more male than female employees use their parental leave benefit.

It's a rare employee who has a baby a year. But an employee who has been given support and flexibility around the birth of a child is likely to return to work happier and more productive, and is more likely to remain loyal to their employer and recommend their workplace to others. In a 2016 study by consulting firm EY of 1500 firms offering paid parental leave, 80 per cent reported a positive impact on employee morale. And 70 per cent reported increased employee productivity.

Parental leave is a prudent investment, in other words. It might cost twelve or more weeks' wages to grant it to an employee, but if it saves you having to recruit and train a replacement, wins you the trust and loyalty of that employee and advertises you as an employer of choice, then the expense starts to look quite manageable.

Now we've reached the part of the essay where we're obliged to talk about Scandinavia. I'm so sorry about that. Really: it's annoying that any time you get even halfway serious about discussing these issues, it's inevitable that – with a heavy sigh – you eventually have to say "Well, of course, in Norway …"

I attended a women's conference in Melbourne in 2017 where the Norwegian ambassador, Unni Klovstad, was a featured speaker. As she outlined the parental leave and child care systems in Norway – forty-six weeks at full pay, ten weeks reserved specifically for the co-parent, child care costs capped at 300 Euros a month – I heard the strangest noise emitting from the women in the crowd. It was a sort of moan of frustrated longing. Almost sexual, to be honest. Most unnerving for the speaker, but fair enough really, given that parents in Melbourne probably burn through 300 Euros a month just feeding the parking meter outside the childcare centre at pick-up and drop-off.

What really interests me in these countries is the way they brought about changes in behaviour by designing parental leave systems that encourage fathers. And not in the "Well, we have a paid parental leave scheme. Just line up over there with all the other mummies" kind of way. I mean in a "Hey you! Yes, you. This is a scheme which you are actually meant to be a part of" way.

In Iceland, there was a significant redrawing of the public paid parental leave system in 2000. Anxious to improve the almost-negligible participation of fathers, the Icelandic government decided to offer families nine months' paid parental leave in total. Three months for one parent, three months for the other parent, and a further three months to be decided between them. The only stipulation is that the birth mother take two weeks immediately after the birth, and the other parent take at least three months; if he or she doesn't elect to take that leave, it's lost to the family altogether. Beyond that, families can decide how they want to manage things, and if both parents want to take leave at the same time, that's fine too.

In 1996, the rate of fathers taking parental leave in Iceland was close to zero. By 2006, the *Nordic Labour Journal* reports, it was up around 90 per cent. Researcher Ingólfur V. Gíslason said that the new scheme had benefits for men and for women, and had led to greater equality in the labour market. And encouraging men to have time alone with their babies helped to address the tendency for fathers to be "helpers" rather than primary care-givers – where, as he put it, "Daddy does what Mummy says." "From a gender equality perspective it is desirable for the father to have the chance to be alone with the baby for a few months," said Ingólfur. "The mother is usually in charge of care when both are at home. But it is good for a father to see just how much work it is to take care of a baby."

Norway, too – as I wrote in *The Wife Drought* – had a significant increase in fathers using parental leave once the model became use-it-or-lose-it. Norway was the first country in the world to introduce a "daddy quota," whereby part of a family's parental leave allocation would only be paid if the father took it. This system was introduced in 1993. In 1992, just 2.4 per cent of eligible men were taking parental leave. By 1997 – four years after the new scheme was introduced – that proportion had shot up to 70 per cent. It's now around 90 per cent, thanks in part to an extension in 2018 that increased the father's entitlement to fifteen weeks at full pay. Now, not all Norwegian fathers take the full entitlement, and there are a range of (from the Australian perspective) rather amusing scholarly articles fretting about dads who only take two months, and so on. But there is absolutely no doubt that intelligent tinkering with national policies on parental leave has brought about profound changes in Norway, both at work and at home. Women's participation in the workforce has increased, and according to the 2019 *State of the World's Fathers* report, Norway is the second-ranked country in the world by ratio of women's and men's under-taking of unpaid caring and volunteer work. In Norway, women do 39 per cent more of this work than men. In Australia, women do 80 per cent more than men. In Japan – by way of comparison – women do 380 per cent more.

More recently, Germany made some significant changes to its "Elterngeld" scheme, which offers a salary substitute for the first year of a child's life. In 2007, the scheme was tweaked to offer a further two months' pay – but only if the "other" parent takes the time off. Before the change, 5 per cent of dads took paid parental leave. By 2014, that proportion had risen to 34 per cent.

I mention these examples not to rub your nose in it or anything, but to make the point that attitudes that seem intractable can actually be changed quite quickly, given an intelligent approach to design. If you know, for instance, that fathers tend to define their value to their families by their ability to provide, then as a policy-maker you need to work with that circumstance. Behaviour in the above-mentioned countries changed quite quickly once legislators recognised that fathers wanted to provide, and worked with rather than against that conviction. The notion that the family would miss out on an entitlement if they didn't take time off was the prompt these fathers needed.

According to this country's Workplace Gender Equality Agency, only 2.3 per cent of Australian men took parental leave in 2018. And while 70 per cent of employers have a policy or strategy for flexible working, only 2 per cent have made an explicit effort to involve men. Which – given we already know that women are good at asking for flexible work, and men are bad at it – makes no sense at all.

I hear what you're muttering to yourself. Fine for Norway, with its towering sovereign wealth fund, to bankroll months of parental leave for all and sundry. Fine for Scandinavia as a whole – with its Nordic aplomb around social welfare payments that would give thrifty Australia a coronary – to embark upon these schemes. But what about countries more like ours?

Okay then. Let's look at Canada. Canada actually has a made-for-social-researchers model, because in 2006 the Quebec region introduced its own new parental leave arrangements while the rest of the country soldiered on using the existing system. The national Canadian system gives dads shared access to leave with their partners, and leave is paid at about half the household's wage, with a strict cap (at present, the cap is around $560 a week). Taking the entitlement leaves many households worse off financially, but it's better than nothing and certainly better than what's on offer in the United States. By way of contrast, Quebec's alternative scheme, the Quebec Parental Insurance Program (QPIP), increased the amount of replacement income and established a five-week "daddy quota" of leave available only to fathers, on a use-it-or-lose-it basis.

Canada is one of those sensible countries that conducts regular time-use diary surveys of its population. These are rather intrusive affairs that ask randomly chosen families to record all their activities for a period, so that a picture emerges of the spending of leisure time, and who does the cooking, cleaning, yard work and so on. These are extremely valuable surveys, because otherwise we have no idea how unpaid work is divided up. You can ask individuals to provide estimates of how much domestic work they do, but if you've ever lived in a share house or a marriage you will be aware how misleading such self-assessments can be. Australia started doing time-use surveys in the 1990s, and very useful they were too, but to the chagrin of social researchers the planned 2013 survey was ditched amid the fallout from the global financial crisis, so we haven't conducted one since 2006. Canada, however, has been keeping up.

Labour economist Ankita Patnaik quickly saw the potential in the Quebec scheme. Because some Canadians were hived off to this new program and others continued as usual, the circumstance constituted a beautifully useful trial with an established control group. And the presence of time-use surveys both before and after QPIP's introduction allowed her to gauge what the knock-on effects of the scheme were for the division of domestic labour. Paternity leave, she posited, might permanently change the balance in a household. She also hypothesised, rather sternly, that "Paternity leave should also limit the possibility of strategic shirking, since fathers cannot credibly claim to lack skills in certain childcare and house-work tasks any longer."

Patnaik found that the results of the scheme were clear: the proportion of fathers who took parental leave surged from 21.3 per cent to 53.6 per cent. On average, participants also took three weeks' more leave than their predecessors had. Patnaik established, fascinatingly, that the increase in uptake was driven not only by the economic incentive of higher benefits, but also by the fact that they were explicitly labelled "Daddy-only." It was, she wrote, an important signpost for men, and a form of explicit permission.

> The label establishes a father's individual right to leave, removes the need to negotiate with his wife, and improves his bargaining posi-tion with employers and co-workers, who may be more sympathetic to him using leave designated for him," Patnaik observed. "Moreo-ver, the quota sends a public message that promotes fathers' involve-ment, which may reduce social stigma against men taking leave and possibly even introduce stigma against those who do not utilize this generous opportunity to spend time with their children ... fathers are more likely to take parental leave if their brothers or co-workers have done so.

Comparing Quebec families before and after the new scheme, Patnaik noted some further striking results. Under the QPIP system, mothers spent an hour more in paid work per day. And fathers who had taken parental leave under the new system spent thirty-six more minutes a day at home, and fifteen minutes a day more on housework, than their counterparts. "The results of this study have important policy implications," wrote Patnaik in her conclusion. "First, they suggest that 'daddy quotas' may help fathers overcome such barriers to taking leave as social stigma and per-ceived professional penalties." Second, she argued, the Quebec experience demonstrated that extending fathers' time at home by as little as three weeks could change the dynamics of a household for years to come.

"Third, and perhaps most importantly, these results suggest that there need not be a trade-off between gender equality and parental investments in children, such that paternity leave may present us with a rare win-win scenario."

This final observation gets very close to the heart of the matter, in my view. The arguments about who advances at work and who does the majority of the work at home are historically encrusted with accusation; it's hard to have this discussion academically (let alone between two tired people in a suburban home, one of whom has just maimed their foot on an abandoned Lego astronaut) without resorting to finger-pointing. And yet it may well be possible to arrive at a solution that is – as Patnaik says – win–win. Where families are able freely to make the choices that suit them, and children maximise time with parents who aren't out of their minds with stress. The Quebec scheme, once again, recognises the needs and pre-existing impulses of fathers and works with them, not against them. Seeing that fathers feel they need to provide for their families, the QPIP model both increased the financial attractiveness of taking leave and made the offer use-it-or-lose-it. The family, in other words, would actively be missing out on something if the father failed to sign up. And by labelling it explicitly, the scheme also addressed the strong tendency among fathers to ignore offers of parental leave, feeling on some level that they are not directed at them.

If you understand why people behave the way they do, then that is the first step to understanding how they might find it possible to change.

CHANGING BEHAVIOUR: SOME CUNNING IDEAS

At a conference a couple of years back, I interviewed Valerie Jarrett, who was Barack Obama's senior adviser for his entire term in office. She told a fascinating story about the early stages of his administration. At meetings, she said, it became evident very quickly that the senior men had no problem making themselves heard, but the women tended to sit back and listen. Jarrett and Obama both noticed this. The solution? Obama invited all the women over for a casual dinner. After the meal, he told them: "I hired you so that you could make yourselves heard for the sake of the people whose interests you are representing. If you aren't able to speak up, then you are occupying the space that could be given to someone who can." Or words to that effect. Quite a brutal approach, on one level, but extremely insightful; in working to correct what is a widely reported female trait (not speaking up), Obama applied pressure using his knowledge of another classic trait (guilt at the thought of letting someone down). Jarrett reported that this intervention brought about a swift improvement to the situation.

Iris Bohnet, in her excellent 2016 book *What Works*, explores behavioural design as a means of bringing about rapid change even in workplaces thought to be set in their ways. By thinking laterally, she explains, one can often come up with an innovative tweak to workplace design that can change the way people think, and thence change behaviour. Sometimes, these innovations can be incredibly simple and cheap. Bohnet's book opens with the story of the great orchestras of the world, which had barely any female musicians until the Boston Symphony Orchestra hit upon the idea of having musicians audition behind a curtain so there was no way of knowing their gender. This simple innovation increased by half the chance of a woman being selected, and thus released a vast talent pool that had previously been unexploited.

Large organisations are hard to run. And if they're trying to turn a profit and deal with myriad changing circumstances – economic conditions, fluctuating markets, layers of regulation – then it's easy to see how often it's administratively simpler to assume your workforce is a static and unchanging resource. That people will work as they always have. One of the greatest forces preventing change in workplace culture around flexible work is inertia. Changing people is hard. Changing culture is hard. But Bohnet's book is an intriguing glimpse of the possibilities of change when organisations take a moment to examine their own assumptions, or come to grips with patterns of behaviour among their employees.

I was at the Women in Mining WA conference a few years back and heard Professor Robert Wood – an expert in organisational psychology who now heads the University of Technology Sydney's Futures Academy – tell a fascinating story of organisational change. The Tooheys bottling plant in Sydney, he said, had many full-time older men who had spent their entire working lives there. Part-time or flexible work was unheard of for these men, which created a problem: upon retirement, they'd go straight from a full-time work week to no work at all – a shock to the system which can be threatening to general health. So the organisation considered – for the first time – offering flexible work and job-sharing to these workers. And it turned out that there were indeed men who were interested in changing the way they worked. Some had family responsibilities they wanted to attend to, some wanted the flexibility to transition into retirement, some wanted to stop doing night shifts. A spokeswoman for the parent company, Lion Nathan, told me that the company first considered changing things in 2015, when it received a request from a factory employee for a job-share arrangement. "This request was unique for Tooheys and was the first such request across the broader Lion Supply Chain," she said. "Prior to that, it was considered too difficult to implement due to the nature of shift work at the factory, which has quite rigid hours. There were also some initial concerns around continuity and team dynamics, as well as part-timers potentially missing out on key teamwork activity."

Tooheys' workforce is 85 per cent male and 15 per cent female. Around half of the employees are fifty-five or older, so the management of retiring men is a significant issue. Executives and management staff at Lion Nathan had already been informally practising flexible work for some years, and the request from the factory floor led to some examination of the unconscious biases underpinning the assumption that the same couldn't work for blue-collar workers. It turned out that flexible work was quite manageable, once arrangements had been made to ensure communication lines stayed open. As of late 2016, across Lion's supply chain more broadly, 35 per cent of male employees and 56 per cent of females had worked flexibly on occasion.

I'm fascinated by stories like these because they demonstrate that, sometimes, baked-in assumptions about how workers will behave can be changed quite quickly, given the right degree of lateral thought.

Here's another. Medibank surprised the market in March 2018 by becoming the first large Australian company to formally abolish the notion of "primary carer" and "secondary carer" in its parental leave scheme. On International Women's Day, the insurer revealed it would offer fourteen weeks' leave at full pay that either parent could take any time in the first two years of their child's life. If both parents worked at Medibank, both could take the full leave – at the same time, if desired. And the company would allow parents to take the leave in one chunk, or two – or even use it to work part-time over the two years. Flexibility was the policy's main selling point.

Group Executive of People and Culture Kylie Bishop said the policy came about as a result of a genuinely open-ended process.

> If I'm brutally honest with you, I'm not sure we were completely clear what we were trying to solve for. We just knew our parental leave policies weren't hitting the mark. Those who were going on parental leave weren't having a great experience, and their re-entry wasn't easy. Our retention rates weren't good – particularly after twelve months. After twenty-four months, we were losing in the region of 70 per cent of those who had been on leave. So we were

tinkering around the edges, looking at length of leave, you know, should we pay super on the unpaid part ... We kicked it around. We asked around ... and what our people kept telling us was, "Look, it's not that stuff. What makes it hard is the big challenge of shared care, making it all work."

So we came up with the idea of doing away with the whole notion of primary and secondary carers. How about we just give people choice and flexibility for shared care?

It was a radical idea. "I used to work in banking," says Bishop. "A few of my former colleagues reached out to say, 'How did you get the business case up?' and I said, 'We didn't do one, actually.' I took it to our CEO and CFO. I said, 'I'm not going to put any numbers in front of you, but I want to talk about "What is the right thing to do? What do we want to stand for?" I wanted this to be an honest conversation, not politically correct, I wanted them to react with whatever they thought." Management announced the policy internally at first. Some reinforcement was needed. "I remember very early on when we launched Family Flex, one of our senior guys came up to me after the session and said, 'So ... the parental leave policy. Is that career suicide?'" recalls Bishop. "He was about to have baby number four. I said, 'Great question, and absolutely not. I'd love to get involved with your story.'"

That senior executive was Andrew Palmer, thirty-nine, who was Medibank's General Manager, Digital. At the time Bishop announced the Family Flex scheme, he and his wife, Christina, were expecting a baby sister for their three young boys, Zachary, Eli and Asher. "My first question was: 'Does this policy apply to senior executives? And if I do take the leave, is it career-ending? Will my job still be there?'" Palmer recalls of that first conversation with Bishop. "Finding a senior role at an awesome company is quite rare. We moved from Sydney to Melbourne so I could work for Medibank. So I felt quite vulnerable. And I wanted to double-check — is this thing real? Because generally in life if something seems too good to be true, usually it is." Reassured by Bishop, Palmer agreed to share his story across the firm's internal communications platforms, becoming a valuable senior role model for other men.

Palmer ended up taking six months off. Because the firm's policy applies to children under the age of two, he was eligible for fourteen weeks of paid parental leave for toddler Asher in addition to the leave for baby Ivy. For his older children, he had taken the standard two weeks' paternity leave. "You've really got to juggle," says Palmer of the two-week arrangement. "Do I take the leave while my wife's in hospital? Do I wait and take it when they come home? And for that time your mind's still on your work anyway; you're in a couple of places at once. No matter whether it's your first or your fourth or your tenth, it's complicated."

Leaving work entirely for a lengthy period of time was a confronting experience at first, Palmer explains. "I found a real separation anxiety when I first took leave. As a man, and a full-time working person, my sense of identity comes from providing – to my job, to the community, to my family. That all comes through work. So the idea of not being there really brings up some questions of who you are, and your sense of value. It's a real fear – 'Well then, who am I?' So, yeah, I found the first couple of months a really interesting journey to go through, getting to the point where I'm not just an employee and a boss; I'm more of a partner and a father."

> Others found it hard to understand too. "I was taking our eldest to swimming classes after school. And there were lots of mothers there doing the same thing, and they had a lot of questions that amounted, in essence, to: 'What are you doing here?' You know, I'd say, 'I'm on parental leave from Medibank for six months.' 'Unpaid?' I'd be asked. 'No, paid, actually,' I'd say. 'Oh. Is Christina at work then?' And I'd say, 'No.' Every question I answered, there'd be another one. And I had some mates saying, 'Well, you've managed to rort the system.' I had some people internally saying, 'Well. You won't be back.'

There's still a stigma around it. I think for women it's expected to take time off. For men it's still viewed as a privilege – it's unusual."

Was the fourth child experience different? "Completely different. I had a few milestones in the six-month period. My second-eldest started kinder, my third started daycare, and I was actually there for those things. Even the small things – taking them to school, being there to talk to them, doing pick-ups and drop-offs – just being an active participant in my children's lives. The biggest benefit was to my wife. Because I was around, she could get back to being more active, and she was able to have a routine."

Palmer is now back at work, but he's changed the way he structures his day. "Now I leave early in the morning and I'm home by 4.30 so I can do the crazy dinnertime, bath, bed routine and my wife can go to the gym. And when Christina's had a tough day at home with the two at home, just knowing she'll have that time out provides a light at the end of the tunnel for her. She says, 'The days are long, but the weeks are short.'"

The arrival of Ivy has been instructive for Palmer in many ways. "To be absolutely honest, before the six months off I kind of knew it was hard but I really didn't know how hard. I'd come home at night and it'd all be done. The boys would be in bed. But that's all changed now. Also, I'd say I'm much better equipped now to deal with mothers who take time off. There's a level of isolation there that I understand much better now."

Back at Medibank, the results of the new policy are startling. Under the old parental leave scheme, only 2.5 per cent of employees taking "primary carer" parental leave were men. "Now, we've just crunched the numbers and it's 28 per cent of those people taking parental leave who are males," says Bishop. "The average time they take is eight weeks." The success of the policy, however, wasn't simply a matter of making the decision and putting out a press release and waiting for the men to sign up. Far from it. Without expressly meaning to, Medibank had prepared the ground by first creating a company culture of openness to the concept of flexible work. When the new parental leave policy was announced, 76 per cent of the workforce was already participating in some kind of flexible work, whether working from home or with flexible start and finish times, or working a compressed week. The company was careful not to associate flexible work only with parents; it promoted flexible work with healthy living, encouraging workers to make time for exercise, or extracurricular interests that kept them happy and motivated. But it wasn't easy. "Flexible work was harder than the parental leave – by a country mile," says Bishop.

Medibank was publicly owned until 2014, when the Abbott government made good on a long-term Coalition promise to privatise it. On 25 November 2014, it was listed on the Australian Securities Exchange. The company moved to a new building; this created an opportunity to change the design of the workplace. "In the old building, everyone had their desk, their plant, their photos of the kids," Bishop recalls. "And the more senior you got, the better office you got, and then when you did really well you got a water view. I came over from the banking sector, and I thought – goodness me."

> But then we moved. We became a listed company and we moved buildings. We were very open in saying that we were moving to flexible work. "No one's going to have a desk. No one's going to have a plant. You'll have to make your own arrangements for your snacks!" And really, the first few months were all about Maslow's hierarchy of needs: we had to address food, shelter and water before we got anywhere near work routine. But then we started talking about flexible work. And we started at the beginning, which meant addressing, quite openly, the basic questions people had, like "How will I know if you're working, if I can't see you?"

These were stubborn perceptions to shift. Bishop brought in an external company to conduct role-playing sessions literally acting out people's concerns. "We made the sessions compulsory, which is something we don't do very often," she says. "My view is, if you don't flush out the conversations, then all you're doing is burying it, and what you end up with is a counterculture." So participants were encouraged to be frank about their concerns: "Someone would say, 'I want to see Joe Bloggs and know that he's at work.' And we'd say: 'Okay. Well, that's a performance issue. Not a flexible work issue.' And so on."

Several issues emerged beyond the basic ones of trust and the convention of presence in the workplace. Some workers felt ostracised because they didn't have children and worried that they'd have to work harder to compensate for parents working flexibly. They were encouraged to draw up their own plans for flexible work, based around other interests or fitness goals. Surprising pockets of resistance emerged. For instance, support staff in the organisation – personal assistants and executive assistants – knew a lot about who was working from home on any given day, or who was dialling in to a meeting rather than attending it. Hot-desking had removed the phenomenon of co-workers eyeballing a colleague who frequently left work early, but there were still gatekeepers who kept tabs on staff movements and passed this information upwards. Bishop realised that extra work needed to be done to win this powerful group of influencers over to the principles of flexible work. "I don't think you can genuinely introduce flexible work and then expect that someone's going to be available to you 24/7," she says. "You've got to try and work out how that's consistent across the organisation."

> A great employee for us is someone who's very comfortable bringing their whole self to work. Who says – I've got these family commitments, or these health goals, and here's how I'm going to make it work so I can be the best Medibank employee I can. This stupid discussion about work–life balance. It doesn't actually exist. As a leader, I would try to customise to make sure I know as much as I can about an individual. You've got to provide a safe environment.

Having waded into the parental leave changes without a specific business model, does Medibank have evidence that the changes are good for business? "In retrospect, it will absolutely be around talent acquisition," Bishop says. "We've already got the numbers around engagement. It's

4 per cent higher among parental leave participants than it is among their counterparts. And we know that our retention rates are much, much higher. Plus, we're attracting more people, because the advocacy is coming not just from our people, but from their families as well."

This word "engagement" is a hugely significant one among big companies competing with each other for quality employees. Medibank – like its competitors – measures the "engagement" of their workforce by asking them regularly whether they feel supported, whether they would recommend their place of work to others, whether they see themselves still working there in two years' time and so on. If your workforce is engaged, you save a whole lot of money training replacements, paying people who are bored or embittered, or throwing around huge bonuses to attract talent from competitors. The fact that parental leave boosts engagement is a serious commercial plus.

Professional services firm PwC introduced an All Roles Flex policy in 2015. The firm adopted the philosophy of "activity-based working." This is a new HR buzz-phrase: essentially it means that the productivity of the employee is assessed on the quality and quantity of the work they produce, not the length of the hours they put in or the extent to which they're physically available to the employer. The change involved a redesign to the workplace, introducing shared workspaces to allow for employees who were sometimes in the office and sometimes working from elsewhere. Now, there are plenty of drawbacks with hot-desking. Not everyone loves it. It suits highly mobile workers, but not people who like to have a plant and a sense of routine. You need to take careful steps to ensure that people who are expected to collaborate can actually find each other, and so on. But there's no doubt that the physical act of moving chairs around can bring about quite significant psychological results, especially for parents.

I arranged to talk to Dorothy Hisgrove, who has the brilliant title "Chief People Officer" at PwC Australia. Dorothy has been a people person at a string of Australian institutions: she was at the AFL before this job, and Australia Post before that, and the National Australia Bank before that.

When I call her, at 9.30 a.m. on a Tuesday, she is at home. "Almost everybody in PwC works flexibly," she says, although: "Granted, I was on an international call at 1.30 a.m." Discussing the firm's transition to a flexible work model, Hisgrove speaks with a passion that is infectious. "Corporates play a damn big role in shaping generations," she says. "It's up to corporates to take the lead on that." Everything that the firm has done is underpinned by a mammoth system of employee engagement and data collection.

PwC measures everything. Gender and diversity representation, comparable salaries, and its employees' responses to all of the above. It measures how many people work flexibly, and how well supported each of them felt doing it. Unusually for a firm of its size, PwC runs comprehensive staff surveys and opens up all comments in real time so they are visible to everyone else. "Every time we survey or pulse-check our people, we receive in excess of 10,000 comments where *all* our people tell it to us like it is," Hisgrove says. "It's really important to measure everything because it's the only way to get change. When you don't hide stuff, it's transformative."

Hisgrove's reference to shaping a generation sounds grandiloquent, until she tells me that PwC's workforce is 75 per cent millennial. The average age of the firm's Australian workforce? Twenty-seven. This has the simultaneous effect of making me feel ancient and sharpening my attention to what she has to say. In recent years, the firm has established gender targets for promotions to partnership and has achieved a 50/50 gender balance in its team leader roles. After speaking to Hisgrove, I check July's announcement of the new PwC partnership round for 2019. There are thirty-one women and thirty-eight men. Flexible work, argues Hisgrove, is a big part of the change, making women feel empowered at work but also creating an environment in which men feel comfortable to leave when they need to.

The old way, where women would drop off at crèche and then arrive at 9.30, with eyes burning into them from everyone sitting nearby – that's gone. With All Roles Flex, we introduced activity-based working. You come into the office, you can sit anywhere. It's taken the stigma away from walking in to the same desk every day. That was the first decision that changed things; it made women feel better about it, and it freed up men to do the same. Now no one knows and no one actually cares, and that's one of the best things about activity-based working.

Today, 86 per cent of the PwC workforce – according to Hisgrove's measurements – work flexibly and report no problems with the arrangement.

And when the firm augmented its parental leave scheme in 2017 to expand its definition of family (foster carers, parents of surrogate-born children and adoptive parents are all eligible), it introduced the concept of flexible leave. "You can take it as a block, you can spread it any way you want or you can do two or three days a week over time." This innovation – for a workforce already conditioned not to be suspicious of flexible work – was the turning point. In 2016, 27 per cent of those taking parental leave (long or short) at PwC were men. In 2017, the figure was 36 per cent. In 2018, it was 40 per cent. And in 2019 to date, of 127 employees taking parental leave, sixty-five were women and sixty-two were men – very close to 50/50.

"Flexible parental leave has proved very appealing to men because they can maintain connectivity at work but they can also be with their children at home at an important time," says Hisgrove. "It's not until people see that there's no adverse impact to their promotability that they think, okay, I really can take that twelve months off. Our men coming back off parental leave are taking to social media and telling their stories. So it's promoting positive workplace culture back to us, which we didn't have to ask them to do. They're talking about how brilliant it is, and how they can maintain their connection to work. Having them talk about it openly on social media platforms drives a lot of change."

Jack Bell, a young father and manager at PwC, posted online about his three months' paid leave with son Charlie upon his return to work.

"I started out thinking of all the wonderful things I was going to do with this 'time off' that normal life doesn't permit," he admitted, of the leave he took while his wife went back to work. "Netflix bingeing, lowering the golf handicap, cooking new recipes, further study, actually reading a book, general life admin ..." None of that got done.

> Not until I was thrown in the deep end on my own did I really learn. Some days we did it all: eating, sleeping, washing, cleaning, playing, outings, shopping and dinner on the table at the end of the day. Some days it just didn't go to plan.
>
> The first year of being a new parent is probably the biggest game-changer most people will ever experience. Your world is turned upside down and the unexpected expenses just keep coming. Financially for our family it wasn't an option to take unpaid leave for this period and to be honest wouldn't have even been considered.
>
> Gone are the days where it's mum that automatically stays home and looks after the kids. My wife loves her career and loves being a mum. Having me at home for the past three months has been the perfect transition for her getting back to work and she has absolutely loved having me at home and the support I have been able to provide. As for returning to work, I'm ready. I'm re-energised and excited to leverage my new skill set and experiences. I'm more patient, organised and compassionate and I know I've got it covered the next time someone spits the dummy. I have new feathers in my cap, and as repayment to my employer for the last few months, I'll be better at my job for it.

Now, obviously Jack is a poster dad for parental leave. And PwC – and any professional services firm for that matter – has a field of enterprise that lends itself to hot-desking or working from home. In some workforces (construction, say, or shopfront retail) flexible shifts might be possible but working from home isn't an option.

Anecdotally, blue-collar men are more likely to respond to work–family pressures by moving to self-employment, allowing them to set their own hours.

The truth is that equality of opportunity for both flexible work and parental leave is coming quicker for well-paid white-collar workers than it will for other workers. "That's why we need to make sure that government is in step with the mood," says Emma Walsh, of Parents At Work. "Leaving it to the private-sector has the effect of improving things only for a certain group." But the history of parental leave in this country tells us that big organisations and governments play an intersecting role in changing culture. Whitlam legislated for paid maternity leave in the public sector and then big private sector employers followed suit and expanded on the theme, gradually normalising the concept of maternity leave to the point at which a public paid scheme could be legislated. Large organisations are now improving by venturing towards the – still minority – view that perhaps there need not be any policy difference between mothers and fathers.

Telstra – a large Australian employer with a varied blue-collar and white-collar workforce, surprised many when, in 2014, it announced a company-wide policy to make every job flexible. In July 2019, it announced that – like Medibank – it would now offer a parental leave policy that made no reference to primary or secondary carers, and would be available to men and women without differentiation. "We will be tracking the take-up with great interest," Telstra's head of diversity and inclusion, Kylie Fuller, told me in an email. "We already have fathers lining up to apply." Fuller's email footer reads: "We work flexibly at Telstra. I'm sending this message now because it suits me, however I don't expect that you will read, respond or action it outside of regular hours."

Big organisations are moving, and that will bring cultural change. Since I wrote The Wife Drought, the developments that most encourage me are the profusion of research into the business case for workplace diversity, and for having a workforce that is permitted to manage their work and lives in a way that makes them happy and fulfilled.

Governments can't legislate to change people's assumptions. Nor can they correct a culture that has hung on to the idea that raising children is women's work well past the point at which it relinquished the idea that earning an income is solely the preserve of men. But there are certainly ways in which governments can help. In Australia, for instance, we could start by rethinking the legislated assumption that the Commonwealth's paid parental leave scheme is for mothers. Currently, the payment is available to all mothers earning $150,000 or less. Claimants can then transfer part of the entitlement to fathers or partners, if that person is the primary carer.

But the birth mother is still the gatekeeper. Which creates some anomalies. For instance, if a woman earns $155,000 a year and her husband earns $40,000, and they decide that the father will be the primary carer, they'll be ineligible for paid parental leave because the woman earns too much to apply, and thus can't transfer the leave to her husband. But in a family where the gender positions are reversed, it's not a problem: the birth mother earns less than the cut-off and is easily eligible.

The simple approach would be to remove the primary carer requirement and make the payment available to all parents. This would, of course, increase the cost of the Parental Leave Pay scheme, which in 2019/20 is budgeted at $2.3 billion. But keep in mind that Australia's is the second-least generous public parental leave scheme in the OECD. Compared to the schemes in other countries, it's cheap.

A less expensive option would be to expand the entitlement and make a chunk of it use-it-or-lose-it for dads and co-parents. This retains the concept of the primary carer, but at least establishes the principle that it's reasonable for fathers to expect more than the bare minimum of a fortnight's leave to cope with a huge change in their lives.

BACKLASH OR BREAKTHROUGH?

This isn't about social engineering. It's about social de-engineering, if anything. Nothing in this essay is intended to suggest that men be forced to work flexibly, or take parental leave. But if you accept – as I do – that our culture presently puts pressure on men not to do these things, then it is a step towards freedom and equality to remove those constraints. If women and men have some sort of instinctive or primordial urge to behave a certain way, then let them do so in circumstances of utter freedom to do otherwise. One hundred years ago, it was uncontroversial to think that women were genetically unsuited to public office; such a view was unchallenged because no woman had ever been elected to parliament. But a century down the track you'd be hard-pressed to find even the most recalcitrant traditionalist who would mount the old arguments that women weren't suited to public office, or were congenitally uninterested.

Women's surge into the workplace has been profound over the last century. But it hasn't been matched by movement in the other direction: while the entrances have been opened to women, the exits are still significantly blocked to men. And if women have benefited from the sentiment that "girls can do anything," then don't we similarly owe it to the fathers, mothers and children of the future to ensure that "boys can do anything" means everything from home to work?

The nagging inequity of men's and women's access to flexible work and leave entitlements carries – moreover – a darker risk in the modern workplace, alive as it presently is with debates about sexual harassment and the representation of women.

In March this year, I hosted an episode of the ABC's *Q&A* with an all-female panel discussing gender and leadership. Towards the end of the discussion, a high-school student called Samuel Mak rose to ask a question.

> Since the #MeToo movement, toxic masculinity has been described
> as male feelings of entitlement, anger and vulnerability, and the urge
> to dominate and intimidate. This has led to a certain amount of

controversy, as it lumps all men as seemingly criminal and also feeds off the idea of male privilege and entitlement, which many men do not believe exists, particularly when we see the differences in legislation with maternity leave and women's priority in family law. I'd like to ask the panel, does this notion of toxic masculinity seem fair, given the amount of guilt and shaming towards one generation of men who have never dealt out any violence?

Various panellists assured Samuel that gender equality was an enterprise for both genders and so on, but I thought about Samuel long after the show was over. How many young men are carrying around this feeling that they are lumped with the transgressions of an older generation, while missing out on entitlements that should reasonably be theirs?

A large survey conducted last year by the 50/50 by 2030 Foundation at the University of Canberra confirms that there is a storm-cloud of resentment building among millennial men. When asked whether they agreed or disagreed that "Men and boys are increasingly excluded from measures to improve gender equality," 48 per cent of millennial men agreed. In fact, of all the generations of men who participated in the survey, the millennials were the group who felt most excluded from the gender equality project. "These results give us significant cause for concern," the authors wrote. "The observation that younger generations of men view themselves as outsiders, actively excluded from what is now increasingly one of the key debates in many workplaces, indicates that there is no room for complacency if we want to avoid a backlash against workplace interventions to address gender inequality."

This study should sound alarm bells among theorists who have always assumed that the younger generation of men would be natural allies of feminism. And it suggests that while millennial dads may well want to be more involved in their children's lives than their own fathers were, they may also be increasingly resentful of the gender barriers that stop them from doing so.

Hunter Johnson, CEO of The Man Cave project, which works with young Australian men, says of Samuel's question: "He's articulated that a lot more coherently than a lot of men, but that's a conversation I see all the time. A lot of men are scared to voice the question because they're scared of being seen as politically incorrect and insensitive." According to Johnson: "Masculinity is in a period of flux. There used to be a collection of rules. But a lot of men are now just horrifically confused. They hear a whole range of mixed signals, all the way from 'Don't be gay,' 'Don't cry' to 'Be more emotionally vulnerable.'" Johnson says it's imperative that young men have the space to talk openly about these questions, including the changes in what might be required of them at work and at home – especially given that the expectations of them as fathers are different from what their own fathers faced. How does a culture learn to respect and reward a man for being a good and connected father, rather than – or as well as – being a capable breadwinner? "The thing that's not often talked about is the conditioning of male pride," Johnson says.

It strikes me that for men, the deliberation around taking parental leave – or working differently to reflect demands of family more broadly – is still characterised by thoughts of loss. How much will it cost my family? How much will it cost my career? How much of myself will I lose? In the Borgkvist study, all the men evaluated themselves by reference to their paid work, not to the caring work they did.

But what about the gains to be made? The men quoted above – given the opportunity to take leave without threat of professional disadvantage – testify as to their improved relationships with their partners and children, and their improved perspectives at work. Taking parental leave early in a child's life – according to a 2014 study of fathers in four OECD countries including Australia – is correlated with deeper engagement with that child later in its life. How heartbreaking it is that care and responsibility for one's own family should ever be identified – in a professional context – with fecklessness or lack of commitment.

For employers, the gains from giving men some flexibility are considerable. Happy, fulfilled employees with families who get to see them, for example. Plus, there is ample evidence that flexible work can lead to greater productivity. In a 2010 global study of IBM workers, for example, it was established that fathers of young children could produce up to a staggering thirty hours more work a week if they were trusted with the flexibility to set their own hours, and the option of working from home.

I started this essay in the world of Australian politics, and that's where I'm going to finish it, with the story of a man who broke the rules and lived to tell the tale.

Tim Hammond is a Perth barrister. He ran unsuccessfully for Labor in the seat of Swan in 2010, then in 2016 was elected to the federal parliament as the Member for Perth, replacing the retiring Labor MP Alannah McTiernan. Hammond entered the parliament on a wave of Labor expectation. Intelligent, articulate and personable, he was appointed straight to the Opposition frontbench and was rated by WA bookies in 2017 as a $4.50 chance to become Australia's next WA-born prime minister. Less than two years later, however, he shocked the place by announcing his departure from politics. As the father of three young children, he said, he was unable to sustain the prolonged absences that the nomadic life of an MP demanded. "When I first ran as a candidate in 2010, I had no kids and Lindsay and I had just got engaged," he explains now. "I saw both a future in federal parliament and having a family. That all seemed entirely workable. What I had no concept of – until I became one – was how profound the impact of being a dad would be on my view of what was important. You've got these little humans who evoke this unstoppable degree of unconditional love. It just really deeply changed my view of what was really important in life."

Work and family did not balance. While Hammond's political career was going brilliantly, his family life suffered. "We had three kids under six, everyone's tired, everyone is completely f…ing miserable," is how he describes it. And while Hammond knew he wasn't the only parliamentary parent struggling with the job's demands, it wasn't an especially forgiving workplace. "The reality is that in today's day and age in parliament – and for blokes in particular – for many, it's kind of all they know," he says.

> Everyone walks around and has that small talk. You know, "How's the kids?", "Oh yeah, it's hard because you're not around" ... for me, the difficulties, in terms of managing the juggle ... were often spoken about in such a superficial way [that] it kind of felt it was making the whole thing worse. It's small talk.
>
> But in another way I think the adversarial, competitive nature of the parliament means that talking about this stuff is to expose your vulnerability. And Canberra isn't a joint where exposing a vulnerability is a very sensible course of action.

In the months before his announcement, Hammond would go for long, intense runs through the pre-dawn Canberra streets, "war-gaming this thing to within an inch of its life." "I was shitting myself about making the decision – coming out, as it were," he says. "I knew as soon as I said it, people would be out hunting for the 'real reason.'" (This sounds melodramatic, but Hammond was right to be worried; in Canberra, when a minister declares that he's quitting for family reasons, colleagues and journalists are as apt to look for an unexploded scandal or pending ICAC investigation as they are to credit miserable spouses or children for the decision.)

> At the time I thought Malcolm Turnbull was going nowhere, I thought that Bill Shorten was going to win, and I thought, I'm probably going to land a cabinet role. That means forty to forty-five weeks a year where I'm not around. My most morbid fear was that having realised I had to jump out of the place, I was just not going to get the chance to find a way out further down the track.
>
> I got to the point where the only thing that was going to work was standing up in front of the country and having this awkward conversation that was the truth: that the whole thing was a disaster.

Hammond duly made his announcement on 2 May 2018, and the world didn't end, beyond general expressions of surprise and a few critics snarking that he should have known what the life involved before he ran for preselection. "But what was surreal was when I was back in Perth, walking down the street and getting stopped by complete strangers who would say, 'Mate, just wanted to say well done, that was a gutsy thing to do,'" he says. "I hadn't expected that at all. It was really something. There's clearly a lot of shared experience out there that isn't getting a run. I'm not even certain that blokes are terribly sure how to set about articulating this stuff."

Hammond counts himself fortunate that he was never the kind of politician who depended on public life as his source of identity or self-worth. "I knew I had a capacity to go back to a career that I found fulfilling," he says. "I can play a role in the courtroom that does make a difference to people's lives. Plus, I get to be home for the unglamorous shitty bits that seem to me to be pretty important."

Hammond says that the most powerful force behind his decision was that "I wanted to be able to look those kids in the eye, when I'm seventy-five and sitting next to the fire with a glass of wine in my hand, and know that I was there when they needed me." But more broadly, he says, Australia is a long way off "making this a conversation that applies equally to dads as it does to mums."

"It's a sweeping generalisation, but I think blokes are not as good at evolving and adapting as women are," he says.

> I don't think blokes lose any of their desire to add value to the family home. But we still take this caveman approach. We still haven't got it through our heads that our true value isn't what it used to be twenty, thirty, forty, fifty years ago in terms of being the breadwinner. Our main way of being of value isn't to be this old-fashioned breadwinner, being out of the house for forty hours a week ... it's to be present with our kids, and our partner if we're lucky enough to have one. It's taking us forever to work that out. Once more of us work that out, the more acceptable it will be to get on the front foot and say, this is what I want.

SOURCES

2   'There are the simple': Angela Shanahan, 'From here to maternity', *The Australian*, 28 April 2018.

5–6   "As a male CEO": Max Schireson, "Why I am leaving the best job I ever had", 5 August 2014, https://maxschireson.com/2014/08/05/1137/.

9   "About 4 per cent": Australian Institute of Family Studies, "Work and Family", AIFS website, https://aifs.gov.au/facts-and-figures/work-and-family, accessed 1 August 2019.

14   "I think people": "Barnaby Joyce on the joys of being a house husband", *The Australian*, 10 May 2018.

16   "Let's take a look at the overview": AIFS, 2019.

17   "the Fair Work Commission in September 2018 ruled": Dana McAuley, "Employers forced to give detailed reasons for refusing flexible work", *The Sydney Morning Herald*, 25 September 2018.

17   "a 2016 study": Melanie Sanders, Jennifer Zeng, Meredith Hellicar & Kathryn Fagg, "The power of flexibility: A key enabler to boost gender party and employee engagement", Bain and Company, 3 February 2016, www.bain.com/insights/the-power-of-flexibility/.

17–18 "Craig and Cameron Zammit": Anna Patty, "Fathers battle to save flexible work hours: Why should parenting responsibilities fall only on women?", *The Sydney Morning Herald*, 25 March 2017.

22   "a 2012 study": Michael S. Dahl, Christian L. Dezs & David Gaddis Ross, "Fatherhood and managerial style: How a male CEO's children affect the wages of his employees", *Administrative Science Quarterly*, 31 October 2012.

22   "a 2008 study": Ebonya Washington, *Female Socialization: How daughters affect their legislator fathers' voting on gender issues*, Yale University, May 2005.

23   "I give the commonsense test": Damien Smith, "Pretty little lady lawyer", Yahoo! News (online), 29 August 2013.

24   "one in twenty is a man": Australian Bureau of Statistics, 4125.0 – *Gender Indicators, Australia, Sep 2018*, ABS, Canberra, 25 September 2018.

25   "42 per cent less": R. Clare, 2017, *Superannuation Account Balances by Age and Gender*, Sydney: ASFA Research and Resources Centre.

27   "What I'm saying to you is": Joe Hockey, interview with Leigh Sales, 7.30, ABC TV, 18 September 2013–21 September 2013.

27   "a rort": Latika Burke, "Federal budget 2015: Arthur Sinodinos criticises paid parental leave sales job", *The Sydney Morning Herald*, 14 May 2015.

29   "a survey in 2017": Adelle Chua, "New fathers reluctant to take parental leave",

18 October 2017, Human Resources Director Australia website, accessed at www.hcamag.com/au/specialisation/diversity-inclusion/new-fathers-reluctant-to-take-parental leave/150856.

30   "In reality": Ashlee Borgkvist, Vivienne Moore, Jaklin Elliott & Shona Crabb, "'I might be a bit of a front runner': An analysis of men's uptake of flexible work arrangements and masculine identity', *Gender, Work & Organisation*, Wiley Online Library, 26 March 2018, p. 709.

32   "a brand-new study": Amanda Cooklin, *Conflicts between Work and Family and Fathers' Mental Health*, report, Australian Institute of Family Studies, June 2019.

34   "among men": Sanders et al. 2016.

34   "Edith Gray's research": Edith Gray, "Fatherhood and men's involvement in paid work in Australia", in Ann Evans & Janeen Baxter (ed.) *Negotiating the Life Course: Stability and change in life pathways*, Life Course Research and Social Policies, Springer Netherlands, Dordrecht, 2013.

37–8 "Like we all do", "I wasn't going to": "Meet the father fighting for paternity leave", video posted on Today.com, 7 June 2019.

38   "I'm a baby whisperer": Emily Peck, "Big bank settles claims that it discriminated against men", *The Huffington Post*, 31 May 2019.

38   "cosmetics giant Estée Lauder": US Equal Opportunity Employment Commission, "Estée Lauder companies to pay $1.1 million to settle EEOC class sex discrimination lawsuit", press release, 17 July 2018.

38   "My employer, Time Warner", etc.: Brigid Schulte, "Journalist Josh Levs forced his employer to give dads more time off, now he wants others to speak up", *The Washington Post*, 15 June 2015.

39   "The culture for men": Jeff Blumenthal, "Dechert fired him for taking paternity leave, lawyer finds", *Philadelphia Business Journal*, 17 December 2010.

40   "landmark report on pregnancy and parental leave": Australian Human Rights Commission, *Headline Prevalence Data: National Review on Discrimination Related to Pregnancy, Parental Leave and Return to Work 2014*, AHRC, Sydney, 2014.

41   "desultory coverage": Doug Dingwell, "Maternity leave is not discrimination, industrial umpire rules", *The Sydney Morning Herald*, 13 October 2018.

43   "when Google": Parents at Work, *Advanced Parental Leave Equality and Introducing Shared Care in Australia: The business case*, white paper, http://parentsandcarersatwork.com/wp-content/uploads/2018/08/PAW_White-Paper-Parental-Leave-Equality.pdf, accessed 1 August 2019.

43   "2016 survey by Deloitte": cited in Parents at Work, 2019, p. 9.

44   "a 2016 study by consulting firm EY": cited in Parents at Work, 2019.

46   "By 2006": Guðrún Helga Sigurðardóttir, "Parental leave in Iceland gives dad a

strong position", *Nordic Labour Journal*, 12 April 2019.

46   "It's now around": "Norway's 'daddy quota' means 90 per cent of fathers take parental leave", apolitical.co, 17 September 2018.

46   "2019 *State of the World's Fathers* report": N. van der Gaag, B. Heilman, T. Gupta, C. Nembhard & G. Barker, *State of the World's Fathers: Unlocking the power of men's care*, Washington, DC: Promundo-US, 2019.

48–9 "Paternity leave:" Ankita Patnaik, "Reserving time for daddy: The consequences of quotas", *Journal of Labor Economics*, forthcoming, written 2 August 2014, p. 10.

49   "The label establishes": Patnaik, 2014, p. 8.

49   "The results of this study", "Because we have a strong relationship": Patnaik, 2014, p. 30.

51   "Bohnet's book opens": Iris Bohnet, *What Works: Gender equality by design*, Harvard University Press, 2016, p. 1.

65–6 "Since the #MeToo movement": *Q&A*, ABC TV, 11 March 2019.

66   "These results give us significant cause for concern" 50/50 by 2030 Foundation, *From Girls to Men: Social attitudes to gender in Australia*, report, accessed 1 August 2019 at www.5050foundation.edu.au/assets/reports/documents/From-Girls-to-Men.pdf, p. 13.

68   "a 2010 global study of IBM workers": Edward Jeffrey Hill, Erin K. Holmes, Jenet Jacob Erickson & Maria E. Ferris, "Workplace flexibility, work hours, and work-life conflict: Finding an extra day or two", *Journal of Family Psychology*, vol. 24, no. 3, June 2010, pp. 349–58.

James Newton

"We didn't get enough votes."

That's what Bill said, smiling bravely into the sun outside his house in Moonee Ponds on what turned out to be the first day of the rest of his life.

It's the simplest, briefest and most true answer to the question all of us whose ambitions for a Shorten Labor government were swiftly and comprehensively terminated on 18 May have been asked by friends and family and job interviewers in the weeks since: where did it go wrong? As one of those casualties, I've taken a keen interest in the various post-mortems. But so far, Bill's answer remains the only one I can completely agree with.

Despite the subtitle of *The Prosperity Gospel*, Erik Jensen is not too proud to say he simply doesn't know why Labor lost or how Morrison won. It's a credit to him and a win for the reader.

Unlike many others, instead of wasting words on pseudo-psephology, Erik gives us telling sketches of the two major-party leaders, their campaigns and the choices Australians faced and made.

There's plenty of the Bill Shorten I like and admire in Erik's interviews and a fair chunk of the Scott Morrison I tried and failed to understand. It might seem a small thing, but there's something chilling about a man who can dismiss the entirety of international fiction by saying he doesn't relate to it and prefers "our stories" while sitting underneath a picture of the Queen and quoting the Bible.

For me, as someone who spent every day of the 2016 and 2019 campaigns on the Bill Bus, the contrast Erik draws between Bill's days and Morrison's was disconcerting. Against Malcolm Turnbull in 2016, we were the plucky insurgency: fun, frenetic, full of colour and movement. In this piece, our 2019 show comes across as earnest but dull. Full of long speeches and detailed pressers, a somehow self-consciously serious exercise. That's not how it felt from the inside. Working and travelling with Bll was very often fun and nearly always funny. But the line that made me sit up and start writing was where Erik describes what we were doing as "betting against modern politics."

Have no doubt: Bill Shorten is a political gambler. He bet on fairness and stood up to the 2014 Budget when some senior colleagues were telling him to roll over. His critics invariably accuse him of political opportunism, yet as Leader of the Opposition he repeatedly chose principle over expediency: on tax reform, marriage equality, climate action and a Voice for Aboriginal and Torres Strait Islander peoples. In 2015, fresh out of the witness stand at the trade union royal commission, he took on his own party over the necessity of boat turnbacks and prevailed. In 2016 he listened to people who'd been ripped off by the big banks and − betting against the Liberals' contempt, powerful institutional opposition and no small measure of internal concern − he got a royal commission. Yet he also recoiled from claiming credit, from overt "leadership" moments, from public rebukes of colleagues or headline-grabbing acts of triangulation. He'd rather win the argument and give his former opponents ownership of the change than take a curtain call. Invariably, he'd scribble over the first few triumphal lines of draft speeches and say, "We don't need to rub their noses in it." That was a gamble too. And, of course, in the breadth and scope of our agenda, we had "ripped up the rulebook" of small-target, low-risk opposition.

For five and a half years, every time we held our collective breath and announced a policy or took a plunge and survived a by-election, a Budget reply or another media-manufactured "test of leadership," I was exhilarated not just by the sense of winning the moment or setting the agenda, but by the thought that we were hammering down another plank in an election platform. Now, eleven weeks into unemployment, I think maybe we were just accumulating baggage for the journey ahead. Perhaps we were using up our luck.

By May 2019, when politics had been skewing to the simple and short-term for years, we were running as the party of complexity. To voters uncertain about the future and suspicious of reform, we offered ourselves as agents of change. With cynicism about politics and democracy rife, we presented a vision for big government activism. Right when we needed it, the zeitgeist deserted us.

Whatever our failures in planning, messaging and execution (and, of course, speech-writing), we didn't do any of this to win a bet. It wasn't an experiment for us, or an academic study. We didn't take on the hard issues, put forward the big ideas and run the campaign we did to prove we were better than the system; we did it because we believed the system needed to be better. But when you combined our new, self-selected complexity with the perpetually complicated mix of emotions, motivations, causes and constituencies that is modern Labor, well, winning was never going to be easy.

Take stability. In the 2016 campaign, Turnbull would occasionally say people had to decide if they wanted Bill to be "Australia's fifth prime minister in three years." Considering he'd only just installed himself as the fourth, it always struck me as a strange argument. But the Liberals never seem burdened by self-doubt. Despite an unmatched record of dispatching Australians to failed wars on bad evidence, they have a superhuman capacity to brazenly assert their status as the natural party of strong leadership, steady hands and a safe country. And as much as we love to say they're out of touch, perhaps they understand better than we do that Australians can forgive a threadbare agenda and overlook a whole lot of grubby scandals because what we crave most of all is the promise of stability — the right to be relaxed and comfortable.

When Bill returned from Christmas at Wye River, he told us how many people had come up to him and, whatever complaint they had about a particular policy, had given Labor "a tick" for being united. Pretty soon he would whittle the line down to: "I don't like everything you're doing, but at least you guys will have the same prime minister for three years." It wasn't exactly "Ask not what your country can do for you," but it had the ring of truth to it.

In early 2014, when I first started working for Bill, any speech that mentioned the Rudd–Gillard governments required a contrite sentence or two about the lessons to be learnt from that time. He became fond of an analogy George Wright had given him about party unity being "the green fee" for national government. Five years later, we had paid the fee and we were proud of it.

Three days of National Conference spoke for unprecedented harmony between the party and the movement. Bill's "stable, talented and united team" rarely missed a campaign mention. Tanya and Penny and Chris and Albo and Kristina Keneally and Catherine King co-starred in the pressers. Hawke and Keating penned a joint op-ed, their first collaboration since 1991. Kevin and Julia shared a laugh at the launch. Short of Mark Latham moving to reinstate Billy Hughes' membership, there was nothing more we could have done to demonstrate our unity of purpose.

Inevitably, commentators tut-tutted about "highly choreographed" moments and "stage-managed" displays, but the Liberals didn't even pretend to go through the motions. Abbott was "too busy campaigning" to come to the launch, Turnbull stayed overseas, not even Howard got a gig. When journos asked Morrison why none of his ministers was doing media, he sneered about not needing people to "prop me up." Again, self-doubt didn't figure.

Of course, for a progressive party trying to take back power, the "stability" pitch could only ever be half our story. The green fee.

Because we were stable, we said, we could be trusted to keep our promises, unlike Abbott. Because we were stable, we wouldn't fracture or compromise, unlike Turnbull. Because we were steady and united, we could end the political dysfunction.

Climate change, we thought, joined the dots better than anything. Any time Bill gave an audience a version of "We won't waste time fighting about whether climate change is real, we'll just get on with real action," he was guaranteed a round of applause. It was a long way from "the great moral challenge of our time," but it had been a long ten years.

With unity and policy, we had a compelling story, and as the man who'd assiduously cultivated that unity, managed the program and driven the "positive alternative" strategy, Bill could bring it to life better than anyone. But it still took a while to tell the tale and, as Bill would say, "explain to people where they fit in."

The town-hall meetings are where people fit in. We'd be in a bowls club bar or the people-mover or a cramped little backstage room with the local candidate kicking around the potential issues and Bill would say to whichever luckless policy adviser was about to be tasked with a hypothetical question on a four-minute deadline: "Mate, I don't want a process answer, I need a real response."

When Morrison gets asked about Newstart, he says, "We believe the best form of welfare is a job." "If pressed," as all politicians' talking points demurely phrase it, he says most people get additional payments anyway.

But that doesn't fly in a town-hall meeting when the person asking the question is living on forty bucks a day — and Bill knew it. He appreciated that the blow-in from Canberra with the white car parked outside can't just airily tell a person who's given up their evening and put up their hand that all they really need to do is have a go.

Bill would start by agreeing that Newstart is too low and explaining that we were not reviewing it to lower it. We need a review because it's a big commitment and there are interactions with other payments and it's complicated and we're in Opposition. But there's a journey to come. He'd talk about the dignity of work and the pain of losing your job and the pressure it puts on family and the harm it can do to community and the need for good TAFEs and employers giving older workers a fair crack and bringing back Aussie apprenticeships and local content and procurement. First question or last, good day or bad, Bill would show the humility, the respect, to give a proper answer. Everyone would be moved to applaud, even those of us who'd heard it twenty times. And when we got back in the car, he'd say, "I need a better answer on Newstart, mate. And on cannabis."

Our gleeful critics have claimed that the breadth of our agenda reflected a presumption of victory. Erik Jensen chalks it up to insecurity. The truth is, we were offering a town-hall answer to every question, nationwide. It was humility, it was respect. If we were asking people to choose us as their government, we believed we had to offer more than a slogan. If we were going to promise new investments in schools and hospitals and child care and pensioner dental, if we were going to eliminate the costs of fighting cancer, then we figured it was up to us to explain to people how we would pay for it.

So, on a whole range of issues, it was the tale of two messages. We were promising stability but asking people to vote for change. We were going to end the chaos but remake the country. We were ready to govern but taking nothing for granted. If there was a phrase I came to dread in the pressers and interviews, it was "please, let me finish."

This kind of nuance wasn't much of a match for endless headlines about "tax bombs," a housing market "collapse" and "class war," and it got us nowhere against the biggest single advertising spend in election history: Clive Palmer's entirely dishonest and almost exclusively anti-Labor, anti-Bill campaign.

I would never actually throw a book across a room, but I got pretty close when I saw Erik quoting a Liberal insider concerned that Palmer was "debasing political advertising." There was only one beneficiary from the wall-to-wall Palmer: the LNP.

We knew the "death tax" campaign was nothing but bad news. What to do about it was another matter. When Chris Bowen and Kristina Keneally went out to smash up the LNP for sponsoring lies, within twelve hours the Liberal campaign had made a video montage of our people saying "death tax."

In the absence of alternatives, we ended up with a position of public contempt and private terror. When, two weeks from election day, my wife texted me saying her colleagues at the hospital were asking her about Bill's 40 per cent death tax, I knew we were in strife.

As for our actual tax policies, by the time of the campaign we'd spent over twelve months talking about closing a loophole that cost Australia more than the government spent on public schools. We called it a giveaway, a gift, a tidy little arrangement, an unsustainable leftover of Howard–Costello largesse. All of these terms pissed off the people collecting the benefit. But nothing cut through with the broader population like "retiree tax."

I watched more of Tim Wilson's committee hearings than was good for me. I learnt the script. When "self-funded" retirees started saying they didn't want to be a burden to the taxpayer, I would sometimes find myself saying, "Well, we've got good news for you!" No one I saw railing against our measures struck me as a true believer lost to the cause, especially those who began by saying "I've voted Labor in the past," as if the next sentence was "but I didn't inhale."

Along with the "death tax," it was the people who would be fine but feared they'd be hurt that broke the heart. A pensioner in the first debate, a vocal passer-by at the Nowra shopping centre, an angry coffee drinker in Adelaide. Never have so many Australians identified so strongly and so wrongly with a tiny percentage of the population.

Then there was Adani. During the Batman by-election, when anyone with a Twitter handle talked about Bill "walking both sides of the street," I tried to cheer up our team by saying that was the only way to knock on all the doors, but in reality we were straddling a barbed-wire fence. Never mind that we couldn't "Stop Adani" any more than we could start digging; in Queensland it swallowed press conferences whole. The tiniest deviation from the language of the previous answer or the previous day or the previous campaign was freighted with imagined significance. Bill was stuck delivering lines, not giving answers. And it showed. I lived in hope that the conservationists would find a more love-able animal than the black-throated finch.

So that's how we spent too much of our campaign. Talking about a mine whose future we couldn't determine, carpet-bombed by ads from a party that couldn't win and didn't care, defending one tax that didn't affect the people concerned and another we weren't imposing at all. Precious minutes of national attention that couldn't be used to tell families about cheaper child care, pensioners about free dental and workers about secure jobs and better wages.

But how could we have changed any of that? Like Erik, I'm not too proud to say I don't know. Apart from collecting around another one million primary votes, I'm not sure what we should have done differently. If we'd promised the spending without the revenue, we'd have been rightly dismissed as trafficking in false hope. If we'd promised to kill Adani, or start construction on day one, half the country would have hated our guts and the other half would have known we were lying. If we'd chatted to Sky before Question Time every day and called in to Jones and gone to New York and kissed Murdoch's ring, they all would have come after us regardless. Nothing we said or did to Palmer would have mattered. Whatever that expression is about picking fights with people who buy ink by the gallon, it's doubly true for a bloke whose ads run right through *Married at First Sight*.

If we'd swapped the town-hall answer for the glib line and abandoned complexity and tucked ourselves into a little ball and said that they'd had three leaders and we'd had one and now it was our turn to drive the car, great swathes of our progressive constituency would have said that we were arrogantly expecting a coronation and that a "Liberal-lite" government was no better than the hard-right real thing.

Finally, I'm poorly equipped to write about "where Labor went wrong" because on so many issues I still don't believe we were wrong. What happened on election day didn't convince me that negative gearing and refundable franking credits are more important than better schools, free cancer care and universal preschool for three- and four-year-olds. Defeat didn't make me think that climate change is a conspiracy or that a Voice will be a third chamber or restoring penalty rates will shutter small businesses across the land. But more than enough people thought differently. In other words, we didn't get enough votes.

So what's the post-mortem? We were brave, we were ambitious, we argued for what was right, not what was easy. No one worked harder than Bill, but a lot of us worked incredibly hard, for many years.

I'll always be proud of the way we went about it, but I wish we'd bloody won.

Or, to use a favourite Shortenism, the operation went perfectly but the patient died.

James Newton

David Marr

Because we got it so wrong, we need to pay particular attention to the 2019 campaign. The *we* is all-embracing: journalists, politicians, punters and the people. Even as the nation queued in May to re-elect Scott Morrison, barely a third of us thought he might scrape home. This is error on an epic scale. Making sense of it matters. Bill Shorten was swiftly consigned to the fat bin marked non-recyclable. Christ and Coal, those very Aussie allies, wasted no time claiming victory. As it has since Hawke's day, the Australian Electoral Study at ANU is doing its exquisite work of matching votes to voters. While we wait for its findings in November, we have Erik Jensen's entirely different approach to understanding what happened on 18 May. His eyes are sharp. Ditto his ears. He asks us to pay fresh attention to what was *said* on the election trail, particularly by Morrison.

It's good to be reminded that Morrison got into the advertising game as a child actor spruiking for Vicks VapoRub. There's a big essay to be written about the damage done to lives and ambitions by too much applause too young. Not now. What matters at this point is that we have a prime minister with a depthless — and not misplaced — faith in jingles. He says: "They stick in your head, don't they?" He never tires of the vaguely decent: "You'll get a go if you have a go." But the jingle that counted most in that long campaign was an old favourite of the man and his party: "Schools, hospitals, medicines, roads – all guaranteed by a strong economy." The key word in that sentence is *guaranteed*.

Shorten's picture of tomorrow's Australia was sketched in detail. His party had policies. He won debates. But Morrison's message – clear, now, when we come back to it in Jensen's essay – was simple: Labor's plans to get Australia back into shape aren't really needed. Prosperity will do the work. No tough decisions have to be made. No one need lose out. Fairness is beside the point. So we'll soon be bleeding $6 billion a year topping up the dividends of the nation's richest investors. So what? We're so prosperous with the Coalition in charge it hardly matters.

First item on the agenda if the government is re-elected: tax cuts for everyone.

The media do a strangely poor job of reporting what politicians say. It's not as if we have to hunt and forage. It's there for the taking. But less and less of what is said makes it to the news. The drift of the press is to cut everything short. This guts argument. Jingles matter more than ever. So little of the key speeches by our leaders go to air these days it's a wonder they bother making them. The great pleasure of *The Prosperity Gospel* is to be immersed in the language of the campaign and reconsider the state of politics in this country knowing that what was dismissed as blather in those weeks worked so well on election day. It's an exercise in hindsight that's not only surprisingly entertaining but speaks with almost scientific clarity. Prosperity was, after all, the only message Morrison preached in 2019 and it came always with the same warning: "Bill Shorten's Labor Party can't manage money."

Pollsters surveying the wreckage of their trade after 18 May argue at least one finding pointed to a Morrison victory: PPM, preferred prime minister. Shorten never closed the gap and Shorten lost. PPM is not infallible, but it's rarely let us down. Contrary to political myth, Abbott even edged ahead of Rudd in the days before the 2013 poll. The wrecker was the nation's PPM. Deep in the figures of all the pollsters, there's another fundamentally reliable figure. It doesn't predict outcomes but measures the perpetual disadvantage Labor faces in federal politics: despite the economic record of the Hawke, Rudd and Gillard governments, Australians are convinced by a wide margin that the Coalition handles money better than Labor. For a few months in 2010, polls showed Labor's struggle to deal with the global financial crisis earnt the respect of the nation. That was a blip. Revisited in *The Prosperity Gospel*, Morrison's speeches and press conferences read as a long riff on this bleak theme.

Why is change so hard in this country? Part of the answer to that perplexing question is Australia's hesitation to trust Labor with the cash box. This isn't a fresh discovery, but Jensen's examination of the campaign just past suggests we need to pay this attitude some serious attention. It survives, year in and year out, despite the mixed economic record of both sides of politics over the past decades. It shapes our politics. I believe it explains why Labor needs particularly charismatic leadership to win government. In 2019, Shorten discovered that putting Labor's policies on the table years in advance and opening a national conversation about the future of the country could be beaten simply by Morrison's message of blather and fear.

David Marr

Judith Brett

Erik Jensen's arresting descriptions of the campaign trail remind us of the many reasons for Scott Morrison's miracle win: Labor's complex policy agenda, Bill Shorten's unpopularity, ScoMo's energetic, self-confident campaigning, Coalition scare campaigns, angry retirees, Queensland regionalism, Clive Palmer's millions, the Greens' foolish anti-Adani caravan, popular local members. Labor's election post-mortems will be exploring them all. The question is: are larger patterns discernible? Here are three I can see.

The first is there in the fact that there are so many plausible reasons, each one making a small contribution to the final result in an increasingly volatile electorate. The Australian Electoral Study has not yet had time to crunch the numbers, but the 2019 election is likely to continue the trend of declining stable identification with the major parties. In 1967, 70 per cent of voters reported always voting for the same party, in federal and state elections and for both houses. In 2016, rusted-on supporters were only 40 per cent of the electorate. Most people are only marginally interested in politics, but with compulsory voting, come election day, they have to make a decision. For the rusted-on, the decision has already been made, but the rest are open to persuasion. So the popularity of candidates has become more important. (How else to explain Tony Abbott's ejection from Warringah, or the success of Helen Haines in Indi?) Particular issues push and pull electors different ways. And how one responds to the leaders seems more significant than ever.

Paralleling the decline in stable partisanship is a decline in trust in politicians and in the popularity of our leaders. Shorten's unpopularity was always going to be a drag on the Labor vote. In deciding whether to vote one way or the other, "I don't like him" is as good a reason as any for many voters. Shorten's problem, it seemed to me, was that he was difficult to read and to identify as a social type. Up against Morrison's public persona of "what you see is what you get," he was at a serious disadvantage. In time, the electoral study will tell us how much. The point, though, is not to find one major cause, or a primary determinant, but to recognise that in a de-aligned and distrustful electorate there will be multiple factors influencing people's vote.

My second larger pattern is the grip mining has on Australia's imagined and actual economy. We are so used to hearing about the Hawke–Keating government's successes in deregulating the Australian economy that we can overlook its failures. In his policy speech for the 1993 election everyone expected him to lose, Keating spoke of his dream that Australia "could become a great manufacturing country, a country which made things for the world to buy. Things which bore the stamp of Australian work and genius. I became convinced that Australia could be more than a quarry and a farm." Keating's bold attempt to free Australia from its historical dependence on farming and mining was doomed by the rise of China, which has decimated our manufacturing industry. We now make even less that the world wants to buy than we did in 1993, and the quarry is much bigger. In 1991/92 Australian exports were 21.1 per cent rural, 25.9 per cent mineral and fuel and 21.4 per cent manufactured products. By 2013/14, minerals and fuels were 50.1 per cent, and rural and manufacturing exports had shrunk to around 12 per cent each. Iron ore and coal are our top two exports, and natural gas our fourth. Keating wouldn't have predicted the third: education-related travel services, including the money overseas students spend on fees and living expenses. But universities scarcely figured in the Coalition's campaign, and only marginally in Labor's. And neither had a plausible plan on how to prepare the Australian economy for a likely global shift away from fossil fuels. Miners and farmers were the symbols of economic responsibility in this campaign, together with the tradies in building and construction which operate in the domestic economy.

The third is the enduring emotional patterns that underpin the Liberal Party's individualism and its policy staples of lower taxes, secure borders and a Budget under control. As Morrison told us repeatedly, he believes in "a fair go for those who have a go," for those who make a contribution and don't just seek to take. This is Robert Menzies' society of leaners and lifters, and Hockey's age of entitlement, though in slightly less accusatory language. It's not so much the self-congratulatory appeal of seeing oneself as a contributor that gives this pattern its power, but the anxieties it evokes: of the never-ending demands that the needy, with the government as their agent, might make on the resources we've each marshalled to support ourselves and our families. Unregulated flows of asylum seekers evoke similar fears.

For many voters, Bill's hand in their pocket, taking, obliterated the benefits of Labor's policies. The hostility to franking credits was out of all proportion to the relatively small number of people affected. It became a generalised symbol of Labor's propensity to tax, while promised benefits such as dental-care subsidies for pensioners barely registered. Morrison made no overt attacks on government-provided services, which would have opened him up to a Labor scare campaign. Nor did he indulge in the demonising of dole bludgers and asylum seekers. Instead, he projected a world of scarce resources, with individuals and families competing with each other to get ahead, and a modest tax refund to reward their efforts. For many unaligned voters, it was enough.

Judith Brett

Barry Jones

Erik Jensen's *The Prosperity Gospel* is a brilliant impressionist account of the recent dismal federal election campaign, full of sharp insights. He had access to Bill Shorten, not to Scott Morrison, but he is both penetrating and balanced. I learnt a great deal from his essay, so I write not to criticise but to supplement.

I expected Labor to win the election, probably by a narrow margin, because I took seriously the results of the normally reliable public opinion polls (and especially the aggregates used by PollBludger). My plants inside the Liberal Party told me they expected Shorten to secure about eighty seats. I anticipated losses in Queensland but thought the ALP would make major gains in Victoria – not quite at the level of Dan Andrews' triumph in the November 2018 state election, but not too far behind. And I was impressed by Bill Shorten's campaigning. He talked in sentences, paragraphs even. He was extremely disciplined and had a very strong front bench.

However, despite admiring Shorten's discipline, I became increasingly nervous as election day approached. In the three head-to-head television encounters with Morrison, Shorten clearly won on substance. He took a long view, with serious argument on complex issues, and showed courage on proposed taxation changes, especially negative gearing and changing the law on franking credits. And yet when Shorten and Morrison met on the ABC with Sabra Lane at the National Press Club, Morrison said nothing, other than repeating his customary mantras about "having a go" and the need to cut taxation, but glowed (assisted, no doubt, by superior make-up), while Shorten made good sense but looked lined and tired.

Morrison proved to be a far more resourceful campaigner than I had imagined, far more effective than Turnbull in 2016. And he was essentially a one-man band. His cabinet, understandably, were hardly to be seen. Morrison seemed to be absolutely tireless and he glowed even more as the campaign went on. He kept on saying "How good is …," then naming the target audience. I could imagine him putting up the election posters, stuffing leaflets in letterboxes, fixing up postal votes all on his own. Where was everybody else?

Fundamentally, Labor allowed Scott Morrison to define the agenda. The role of attacker and defender was reversed. I congratulated Shorten for not running a negative campaign. My judgment was wrong there. He should have attacked the conflicted, confused or deceitful set of ministers in a non-performing government. Scandals such as the water buyback fiasco, the huge gift to the Great Barrier Reef Foundation, relations with the travel company Helloworld, the invisible Minister for the Environment, conflicts of interest and shameless pork-barrelling — all were virtually ignored.

Oddest of all, when the Coalition, with exceptional chutzpah, was insisting that Labor was incompetent with money, Shorten could have responded: "Hawke and Keating created the modern Australian economy and twenty-seven years of constant growth has been based on Labor's work. The Rudd government's response to the global financial crisis in 2008 is generally regarded as having been the world's best and in the Rudd–Gillard–Rudd years Australia retained its AAA credit rating from all the international agencies." But he never made these points. I kept texting to ask why, without receiving a reply.

The Coalition was not challenged about its gross policy inadequacy and toxic personal relationships, succinctly defined by Kelly O'Dwyer as "homophobic, anti-women, climate change deniers." Instead, the Labor Party was under constant, well-funded and wildly exaggerated attack for its ambitious program, as was Shorten as leader. The old political adage "disunity is death" did not seem to apply this time.

The elections in 1969, 1972, 1974, 1975, 1980, 1983, 1993, 1998 and 2007 dealt with complex, sophisticated issues, including foreign affairs, the environment, law reform, creating an open economy, ending White Australia, land rights for Indigenous Australians, and taxation. Whitlam, Hayden, Hawke, Keating and Rudd were serious thinkers. In the 2019 poll, voters responded to Scott Morrison's dire warning: "This is not the time for change." Although the Australian electorate now includes 6,500,000 graduates, the most highly qualified cohort in our history, it is clear that many Australians prefer not to address complex issues in politics. At least, not now.

Morrison's appeal was to the "quiet Australian," a variant of Richard Nixon's "silent majority." Morrison's "quiet Australians" can say, "I have never advocated mistreatment of indigenes or racism or misogyny or wage theft, but I have never said or done anything to oppose these things either."

The Clive Palmer–UAP advertisements, plastered across the wide brown land, charged that Labor would impose "trillions" of dollars in extra taxation and generated fear, especially among older voters, who felt their thrift would be punished. This was essentially a $60 million gift to Morrison, but I doubt if he will list it in his electoral expenses return.

I was concerned that Morrison adopted some of Trump's techniques, not just the baseball cap, but also the use or misuse of language, relying on photo ops, sound bites and mantras. The language was simple, stripped of meaning, but endlessly repeated, again and again, over and over, on and on. At least Morrison generously let Palmer have the slogan "Make Australia Great" (why not "Again"?).

As a religious person (in this, unlike Trump), Morrison has an oddly casual approach to the truth of a proposition. He is essentially a salesman, a Willy Loman. In an age of retail politics, the fundamental issue for him is "Will it sell?" And he was flogging a single product: short-term self-interest.

His ludicrous journey to Christmas Island, with a bevy of media, in March 2019, was based on the proposition that passage of the Medevac legislation would result in an upsurge of refugees arriving by boat. When that didn't happen, the next we heard of Christmas Island was in the April 2019 Budget, with costings for closing down the detention centre. In just three weeks, Christmas Island had gone from being essential to being pointless.

Morrison has routine techniques for evading questions: he either ignores what he is asked and answers something else, or he says, "That's only of interest inside the Canberra bubble." He invariably fails to take responsibility for errors, failures, mis-statements or exaggerations. If anything has gone wrong, it is never his fault: he was away or was poorly briefed.

Even worse was his use of exaggeration, fear-mongering, half-truths and lies. A cynical defence was offered by Morrison, that Shorten's campaign in 2016 against possible changes to Medicare, dubbed "Mediscare," meant that truth was no longer a tradeable commodity in election campaigns. Like Trump, Morrison could say anything – and get away with it.

Also like Trump, Morrison's limited vocabulary helped him win. He kept repeating the words and phrases "hard-working Australians," "work," "home," "family," "How good is … ?," "humble," "quiet," "reward," "amazing," "the greatest country on earth" and "the Sharks." One can be confident that among the words Morrison would rarely if ever use in a campaign are "environment," "global," "planetary," "nature," "creativity," "imagination," "understanding," "explanation," "science," "research," "evidence," "books," "art," "music," "beauty" and "moral leadership." He has his own interpretation of "freedom."

Again like Trump, Morrison seems to be completely lacking in curiosity. On issues raised with him, he either knows the answers already, or has no desire to hear the cases for and against a proposition. He was caught on television on a drought-ravaged farm: "Linking the drought with climate change? Well, that's not an issue I have thought about very much ..."

The campaign was infantilised by Morrison's televangelism. But it clearly worked.

Labor, with its heavy emphasis on attacking "the big end of town," was essentially campaigning against Turnbull, not Morrison. While Peta Credlin's phrase "Mr Harbourside Mansion" had proved lethal against Turnbull, Morrison appeared to be relentlessly suburban in his interests and aspirations.

Ironically, Labor did comparatively well with the "big end of town," affluent seats with high numbers of professionals. Fiona McLeod gained a 9 per cent swing in Higgins, Josh Burns 5 per cent in Macnamara, and there were significant swings to Labor in North Sydney and Bradfield. (However, in lower socio-economic status seats, the ALP suffered heavy swings. Joel Fitzgibbon, in Hunter, had the biggest swing in the nation against him: 14.1 per cent.)

Both leaders had a stroke of luck in the campaign, and neither was asked very probing questions on sensitive issues. Morrison was not asked about his Pentecostalism and the "Rapture," in which true believers are hoovered up to Heaven. Did reliance on divine providence account for his indifference to climate change? Bill Shorten was not asked about the role of factions in the ALP, how they operated as patronage machines, his role as a player, or his hostility to democratising the party.

Shorten bravely declined to meet Rupert Murdoch before the campaign began, and he refused to be interviewed by News Corp outlets or by radio shock-jocks. He paid dearly for that courage and was subject to unrelenting attack, much of it personal. It must have seemed that he was engaged in a fight against Morrison + Palmer + Hanson + Murdoch.

A man, unknown to me, spoke to me at a tram stop. He began, "This is a really terrible government and they ought to be defeated heavily." He then gave a forensic analysis of its failures. (Perhaps he was a barrister.) But his final words to me were, "But I can't stand Bill Shorten. I suppose you'd have to put me down as a swinging voter." I had similar experiences several times a day, throughout the campaign. I found it disturbing because I did not fully understand it, even after mounting a defence.

There seems to be an iron law in politics: for the past hundred years, the first Opposition leader chosen after a change of government has never gone on to become prime minister.

On climate change, Shorten was crazy-brave, proposing significant increases in emissions reductions without explaining adequately why a Labor government would be doing this. Labor's courageous climate change policy was poorly argued, failing to involve millions in the community who engage directly with the issue (gardeners, farmers, bushwalkers, anglers, bird watchers, whale watchers, bee-keepers, skiers, vignerons). Their lived experience and direct observation should have been harnessed, but was not. Shorten never talked about the science, and he rejected my advice to emphasise that each tonne of coal burnt produces 3.67 tonnes of carbon dioxide, which hangs round for decades in the atmosphere as a green-house gas. It is not "demonising" coal to point this out. And he never referred to cement, cows or cities, all three presenting central difficulties in reducing green-house gas emissions. He talked about electric cars, but not persuasively. And he invited criticism that he was straddling the fence on Adani and not wanting to offend the CFMMEU, which had provided him with critical factional support.

Labor was also courageous in promising to end distortionary taxes. But Shorten failed to explain the moral justification of taxation as the price we pay for civi-lisation, with expanding demands, not just in infrastructure but at the personal level: sharing the costs of education for the young and health care for an ageing society, with a contracting revenue base.

The results of the marriage equality voluntary postal survey in November 2017, followed by unprecedented levels of enrolment by young people, gave a false optimism that Australia might be prepared to support courageous changes. Peter Dutton's seat of Dickson voted 65 per cent for "Yes" and he was targeted by GetUp! Surely he must be at risk? Well, he wasn't. Jensen quotes an astute observation by the Liberals' Tim Wilson: "In the same way that kids told their parents how to vote in the marriage equality postal survey, we saw parents tell-ing their kids about the cost of voting Labor."

Bob Hawke's death, two days before polling, produced a powerful emotional reaction, with extensive coverage of ALP triumphs. I thought it might impede any move back to the Coalition. It did not. Morrison handled it very well. Shorten failed to benefit from the mood of goodwill – and that was tough for him, because he admired Hawke greatly.

The final result can be interpreted in several ways. The Coalition won 51.53 per cent of the two-party-preferred vote, the ALP 48.47 per cent, so if three voters in 100 had changed, Morrison's much-vaunted mandate would have disappeared. So that looks like a close result.

The ALP won a majority of seats in New South Wales, Victoria and South Australia, all the seats in the ACT and the Northern Territory, and (with

Andrew Wilkie) progressives won Tasmania 3 to 2. The election was lost in the outlier states of Queensland and Western Australia.

However, the result was not good for the party I have belonged to since 1950. Its primary vote fell to 33.3 per cent. When Gough Whitlam was heavily defeated in the 1975 election after the dismissal, the ALP's primary vote was 42.8 per cent. A figure in the low forties would now seem like a triumph!

A major problem for Labor is its low level of engagement with the community. Can a party with a contracting base (union-controlled factions; small, ageing branch membership) and Senate candidates whom nobody has ever heard of, handpicked by the factions, reach out to an expanding population?

Barry Jones

Elizabeth Flux

Of all the visceral, excoriating lines and vivid imagery in Erik Jensen's *The Prosperity Gospel*, for me it was "Shorten's gamble is that you can replace popularity with policy" that delivered the biggest punch. It gets to the crux of how Australia's political system is broken. Based on how our country voted, Australia both hates itself and is in extreme denial about what we need to do to prepare for the future.

On election night, when it became evident that despite the polling and predictions, it was going to be a Liberal win, I switched channels and ended up watching *Sliding Doors*. It was a weirdly apt piece of programming – a film that splits in two after one moment changes the course of a life. It makes you ask: what if? I wondered briefly what the sliding doors moment was for Labor – if there had been just one, or perhaps a few, that tipped things the wrong way for them. Later, what *The Prosperity Gospel* made clear to me was that there was no one moment. The loss was an inevitability.

This year is the first time I was really awake for an election. It's not that I wasn't engaged before, but previously an election has got into my mind through osmosis. I think that's the normal experience. You can't help but absorb the key phrases, the vague promises, the controversies. You get an overview, a flavour – which I think is all most politicians want you to get. They don't want you to dig deeper, because, usually, there's not much beneath the surface. This year's election was different for me. For the entire campaign period, I was employed as a subeditor with a focus on Australian politics. I not only read article upon article dissecting promises and proposed policies, I fact-checked them, read up on history, and felt I knew exactly what was going on and what would happen. I was well informed and there was no doubt in my mind: Labor would win. Shorten's was the only one of the two major parties that actually had any policies. Morrison was all sizzle, no sausage, but, ultimately and depressingly, 100 per cent democracy.

I'd forgotten – or perhaps until this year hadn't fully accepted – that it isn't about who would do the best job or even who has a plan for what comes next. It's about sales. Who comes off the best. And, as Jensen points out, Morrison is a trained salesman.

Although we don't have a president, and although, in Australia, who leads the party really doesn't matter on a day-to-day level, personality and charisma still carry more weight than actions and promises. It's also not about who's the better person – it's about who puts on the better show.

We remember fondly past prime ministers who were good at the cutting remarks, the quips, the ones who could down a yard of ale in world record time. The "larrikins." But being charismatic doesn't mean you can't also be a good leader – in an ideal world, you'd be both. But it is a bleak fact that if the voters have to choose between these two qualities, they'll pretty much always go for the former.

What is more important when it comes to choosing someone to lead, to represent Australia on the world stage? That they be genuine, or that they simply be good at appearing genuine while playing a role carefully workshopped to appeal to the greatest number of voters, irrespective of what is actually best for the country? From both the election result and Jensen's essay, the answer is clear.

This is the problem with personality-driven politics. Humans vote for human stories, not hypotheticals. Jensen's essay taps into the human details that might otherwise slip through the cracks. He homes in on how Morrison speaks to individuals – through his use of first names, of anecdotes – while Shorten focuses on the bigger picture. It's easier to see ourselves as individuals than as part of something bigger – and so the things that matter don't matter unless they have a direct impact on us. People don't tend to vote with a utilitarian mindset, and Morrison knew this, while Shorten bet on the goodness of humankind – a big mistake.

Based on the election results, the voting majority don't consider the future or are in strong denial about the action that needs to be taken immediately (climate change) and don't look beyond themselves (retirement tax, Adani). So how can tough calls that require sacrifice for the collective good ever be made?

The Prosperity Gospel has helped me understand why I found the election result so difficult to come to grips with. It wasn't that "my team" didn't win. Or that I liked Shorten more. It's because it wasn't a case of one side's policies winning over the other's. People were happy to vote for no policies at all, because we'd rather have a strong man selling nothing than a quiet one trying to make changes which he truly believed were for the better.

In the simplest of terms, what do we really need from a prime minister? Someone who fights for what they believe is best for the country – and whose views represent the majority of the voting public. But the majority of the voting public chose a man who only made vague statements and hid behind glib slogans. As Jensen put it: "The struggle with Morrison is to know what he wants, other than to be prime minister."

When a job comes with money and prestige, there will always be people who will want it purely for these reasons and not because they want to do good. Our recent history of leadership spills is example enough – no one honestly believes that each figure with a knife in their hand betrayed colleagues for the love of their country.

So what can we do about this? Strip away the money and perks? Make the job less appealing somehow? Find ways to make the prime ministership more of a vocation and less of a prize?

Realistically, I don't know that anything can be done. This scenario has played out again and again and I feel embarrassed that I thought this time would be any different. Next time it will be the same. It doesn't matter who is more genuine, honest or well-prepared. The better salesperson will win every time. Morrison's victory has demonstrated this starkly.

I agree with Jensen's conclusion that Shorten represents Australia and that in the end Australia didn't want itself. It wants the idea of itself, and that is what Morrison is selling – a moment in time, rose-tinted, artificial and not sustainable.

Elizabeth Flux

Kristina Keneally

Scott Morrison made prosperity conditional on effort when he said, "If you have a go, you will get a go." Bill Shorten asserted that prosperity is an opportunity to which all people are entitled: "We believe in a fair go for all." Scott Morrison is a Pentecostal Christian; Bill Shorten is a Jesuit-educated former Catholic. It may be crude Christian theology and even cruder politics to say this, but here I go: there is possibly no more perfect contrast between the Prosperity Gospel and Catholic social teaching than Morrison versus Shorten on the Australian "fair go."

When I saw the title of Erik Jensen's Quarterly Essay, *The Prosperity Gospel: How Scott Morrison Won and Bill Shorten Lost*, I thought Jensen might be examining how the tension in these two strains of Christianity is playing out politically in 2019. He didn't. Not directly, anyway. Through a series of vignettes, Jensen sketches the personalities of the two men who put themselves forward to be prime minister and draws conclusions about each one's character, religious beliefs, self-understanding and electoral appeal.

Jensen's writing is superb and his insights perceptive. But I found the essay unsatisfying in three key areas. First, while Jensen introduces the distinctly different religious foundations for each leader's policy and political approach, he does not wrestle with what it means that Australia voted for one over the other. He concludes that Australia "found comfort once again in a hardman who says everything is simple and some of you will be okay" without exploring why. The essay did not live up to its title: it did not really examine how the Prosperity Gospel pitch won. Second, Jensen's profiles of Morrison and Shorten are incomplete, or at least unbalanced, because Shorten agreed to be interviewed and Morrison did not. This isn't the author's fault, but it does mean his conclusions about Morrison must be qualified. Third, he could have explored the role religious affiliation and identity played in the election: in a country where politicians – including Howard and Keating – have typically sought to keep their religious faith private and separate from their political lives, does Morrison's explicit, on-display Pentecostal faith signify a deeper shift in the electorate's openness to the role of faith in the public square?

Let's deal first with the theological basis for Morrison's "If you have a go, you'll get a go" versus Bill Shorten's "A fair go for all." The Prosperity Gospel, which Jensen asserts Morrison represents, emphasises Biblical passages that promise individual blessings, such as health and wealth, to people who believe in Jesus Christ: "My God shall supply all your need according to his riches in glory by Christ Jesus" and "Beloved, I wish above all things that you may prosper and be in health, even as your soul prosper." The Prosperity Gospel is most often proclaimed within Protestant and evangelical churches. These traditions insist that an individual can cultivate an unmediated, one-on-one relationship with God. Individuals can receive divine revelation: a person can come to know Jesus Christ simply by reading the scriptures and accepting Jesus as Lord and Saviour. The call to holiness is a personal invitation from Jesus to convert to right living. The person who makes this conversion – who believes in Jesus, reads the Word of God in scripture, prays, and lives by the Bible's commandments – will have good fortune bestowed upon him or her.

Adherents to the Prosperity Gospel often cite Jesus' telling of the Parable of the Talents. In that story, a master gives three of his servants an equal sum of his fortune to manage. One buries it, earning no interest but returning the original amount safely to his master. The other two invest their shares, and are able to return the principal plus interest to their master. The master admonishes the servant who played it safe and rewards the two servants who took a risk and increased his wealth. In this parable, we can recognise the premise of Morrison's political pitch: if you have a go, you will get a go.

Catholic social teaching finds a different meaning in the Parable of the Talents, interpreting its message as an exhortation to use one's talents and wealth in the service of others, even if it means risking a loss. It reads this parable alongside others, such as the Parable of the Good Samaritan, and in the context of Jesus' commandments to feed the hungry, clothe the naked, care for the sick, visit the imprisoned and console the sorrowful. Throughout the Gospels, Jesus locates himself alongside the poor, the outcast, the marginalised and the powerless, and calls on his followers to act in ways that improve the lives of oppressed people: "Whatever you do to the least of my brothers and sisters, that you do to me." Jesus' call to care for others is not conditional. As the Parable of the Good Samaritan shows, we are not to ask someone to "have a go" before we act to help them. We are to respond to their inherent human dignity. Reading the gospel in this context, Catholic social teaching asserts that Jesus insists on a fair go for all.

Catholic social teaching is a rich and deep tradition in the Christian church. It reaches back to Augustine and Aquinas, is given expression in papal encyclicals such as Leo XIII's *Rerum novarum* and John Paul II's *Centesimus annus* and is recognisable in the practical work of people like Dorothy Day, Mother Teresa and Oscar Romero. It is central to Catholicism, but its emphasis on social justice is recognisable in other Christian denominations too, such as the efforts by the Uniting and Baptist churches to help marginalised people by providing charitable services and advocating for funding or laws to address poverty, family violence or drug addiction. Importantly, Catholic social teaching promotes collective social action for the common good, just as Catholic theology insists that divine revelation is received by the church as a whole, not by individuals alone. This is what is known as the *sensus fidelium*: a universal truth is known when the whole of the faithful recognise it and give it their assent. This emphasis on collectivism over individualism is one of the factors that sets Catholicism apart from Protestantism.

Here's the question I had hoped Jensen's essay would explore: why, at a time of rising inequality, growing intergenerational inequity and significant economic uncertainty, is the electorate more strongly attracted to the Prosperity Gospel pitch than the Catholic social teaching platform? Whether it is unemployed and poor Americans voting against their economic interests for Donald Trump's corporate tax cuts, UK citizens opting to go it alone with Brexit, or even the fact that Jordan Peterson's *12 Rules for Life: An Antidote to Chaos* is a runaway hit, there is ample evidence that first-world citizens are drawn less to an appeal to collective social action to overcome injustice and more to claims that individual effort will *always* reap its own rewards.

It may be that at a time when institutions are failing ordinary people – the banks are ripping off customers, religious organisations are abusing children, government seems incapable of doing anything about stagnant wages or rising power prices – people conclude that their best option is to look after themselves because they can't rely on organisations and institutions any longer.

Then there is the simplistic explanation favoured by some media outlets in Australia, which is to claim the political left are infatuated with redistribution and just don't get aspiration. That argument is not only absurd, but also ignores that there are real social and economic barriers to accessing education, housing, healthcare and jobs – making it harder for people's aspirations to be realised. Yet the Prosperity Gospel pitch for individual effort seems to magic those barriers out of existence in our political debates, and keeps succeeding electorally. Why? I was disappointed that the essay barely touched on this question.

Instead, the essay is more an examination of the personalities of Morrison and Shorten. Using what he had, Jensen did capture to some reasonable extent the theological bases that frame the two men.

Bill Shorten was raised a Catholic and educated by the Jesuits in Catholic social teaching. "Be a man for others" is the Jesuit motto. Shorten's life is dedicated to collective social action for working people. He knows injustice holds people back – he saw how poverty and sexism denied his mother the opportunity to live up to her true potential. He wanted to lead a government that removed such barriers.

Yes, Shorten has doubt – plenty of it. In wide-ranging one-on-one conversations with Jensen, Shorten contemplates whether God exists, whether there is a heaven or hell, and whether he has what it takes to be prime minister. Jensen says such doubts indicate Bill Shorten doesn't know who he is. I have a different view: Shorten may have doubts and faults, as we all do, but he knows who he is in relationship to others. He is a collaborator and he grounds his identity in his relationships. As leader, Bill preferred to locate himself among his team. I dare say that Bill would agree that the greatest disappointment from the election is not that he isn't prime minister, but that the Shorten Labor team didn't get to form government.

Morrison, on the other hand, put himself forward as an individual leader, and wanted no one from his team around him. He pitched himself as the saviour of his party. Morrison is a Pentecostal Christian. He speaks openly about his faith. He prays. He considers his life marked by blessings and miracles. He appears to have a deep and intimate relationship with his Lord, and draws inspiration and guidance from his Christianity. It gives him a certainty, perhaps, maybe even a salvific mission and sense of destiny.

Jensen describes Morrison as a hardman who says everything is simple. Doubt, of the type expressed by the apostle Thomas after Jesus was reported to have risen from the dead, appears not to be a feature of Morrison's faith or personality. Or maybe it is. Who knows? Unfortunately we don't, because Morrison refused to be interviewed for this essay.

Jensen observes that ambition comes from insecurity or privilege. He asserts that Shorten is insecure and would have governed from that insecurity. Jensen likewise implies that Morrison is secure and confident in who he is and what he believes. But can we really know that Morrison is this confident? Morrison's unwillingness to answer questions – an unwillingness he shows not just with Jensen, but in his press conferences too – might just indicate a lack of confidence to engage in complex discussion. Perhaps his bellicosity masks deeper doubts? Is Morrison's confidence play an act?

I also wish Jensen had been able question Morrison on his understanding of the gospel message. For example, Jesus is pretty harsh on the accumulation of wealth: "It is easier for a camel to pass through the eye of a needle than for a rich person to enter the kingdom of heaven." How does Morrison interpret that, and how does it affect his political agenda? What does Morrison make of the Parable of the Talents? What does he think is the message for contemporary Australians in the Parable of the Good Samaritan? Jesus didn't distinguish between the deserving and the undeserving poor. How does Morrison square that with "If you have a go, you will get a go"? In the end, because Morrison declined to be interviewed, these questions were left unasked and unanswered.

Finally, the essay left me wondering if Jensen sees any significance in Australia having elected a prime minister who speaks like an evangelical preacher and who puts his worship on public display. As a politician who has been often criticised for bringing my faith into the public square, I am equally bemused and confounded by this development. Is Australia really undergoing a shift in its attitudes towards religion and politicians? Census data tells us that atheism is on the rise and religious practice waning, but are we somehow growing more at ease with political leaders professing faith overtly? I'm comfortable if we are, but I am not yet convinced that is the case.

Did religion and faith matter, or not, in this election? Would a showman making the same simple pitch, with a bit of scaremongering thrown in, and minus the religious elements, have resonated just as well? The essay doesn't grapple with these questions. But grapple we must. Almost every media outlet, all betting agencies, most polling agencies, most Labor MPs and even a large chunk of Coalition MPs didn't believe Morrison could win. Was his victory really a miracle, or just something more prosaic?

Kristina Keneally

Patrick Mullins & Matthew Ricketson

In October 1996, the British historian Anthony Seldon published a survey of Tory governments in the UK since Pitt the Younger. The timing was apt: by identifying the factors common to the demise of all those governments, *How Tory Governments Fall* provided a checklist for those watching the Conservative government of John Major as it tottered towards a landslide defeat at the hands of Tony Blair's Labour Party. Confusion over policy direction and palpable internal disunity? Check, check. Straitened finances and disarray in the party organisation? Check, check. A hostile and intellectual press climate? A loss of confidence in the party's capacity for economic management, a sense that it is time for a change? A rejuvenated and credible Opposition? A negative image of the party leader? Check, check, check, check, check.

Though individually they verge towards truisms and clichés, the sum total of these factors constitutes a framework by which to understand the loss of conservative governments – and not merely those in the UK. Applied to Australia, this framework helps to make sense of the Howard government's 2007 loss of office, the Fraser government's 1983 loss and the McMahon government's 1972 loss. It also helps us understand – admittedly, more in hindsight – that the likelihood of an election loss for the Coalition parties in 2019 was much more remote than consensus had it. The Coalition used forecasts of a Budget surplus to sandbag its claims to superior economic management; it stoked concerns over franking credits and negative gearing policies to damage Labor's public credibility; and it muffled criticism of policy inconsistency and disunity by consigning it to the "Canberra bubble." The Liberal and National party organisations were neither straitened nor in disarray, and the apparent mood for change that was so pervasive and absolute when Malcolm Turnbull was deposed seemed, by May 2019, to have dissipated. Press consensus that the government was likely to lose did not prevent an ongoing fusillade against Labor from the News Corp papers. Most important, perhaps, was the advantage Scott Morrison enjoyed when the choice came down to the image of the party leader: "You vote for me, you'll get me," Morrison said. "You vote for Bill Shorten, and you'll get Bill Shorten."

Erik Jensen's Quarterly Essay does much to illuminate that choice and the kinds of images that both leaders projected over the course of the election campaign. One of the most acute points to emerge from the essay is Morrison's professional and disciplined delivery of a clear message. His press conferences were short, taut affairs, with few opportunities for distraction or digression. His interactions with journalists were brisk. His language was simple and straightforward, with few (if any) verbal flourishes. The images and the audio were highly conducive to grabs for nightly television screens: familiar, cheery, colourful, simple. It was ordinary stuff, extraordinarily well done.

It represented a successful play on the disregard Australians have long held for politicians and those on the "inside." By relentlessly broadcasting his ordinariness – with the baseball caps, the refrains of "Have a go, get a go," and the over-proud support for the Sharks – Morrison presented himself as a regular Australian, average and everyday. By invoking principles of hard work and dignity, by referencing family and community, Morrison fused himself – as Jensen says – to John Howard and Robert Menzies, and thereby tapped into ready-made tropes of suburban, middle-class Australians as forgotten, as battlers, as "quiet." Taking advantage of the widespread regard that he was the underdog, Morrison positioned himself as the champion of the disenchanted and overlooked. And by the constant claim to be exactly what he appeared and nothing else – dutifully spouted by those close to Morrison, and recorded by Jensen: "What you see is what you get" – Morrison drummed in the message that he was authentic, not of the Canberra bubble that he so regularly dismissed.

He was helped by the contrast with the Labor leader. The mid-2000s regard for Shorten – the faint-haloed hero of Beaconsfield – had long since faded. Thanks to his role in the Rudd–Gillard–Rudd years, Shorten had become synonymous with duplicity and treachery. For all his work with the AWU and his record as a minister, Shorten, as David Marr put it in his 2015 Quarterly Essay, *Faction Man*, is "seen as a shape-shifter, driven entirely by politics." Every seeming hint of inauthenticity during the 2019 election campaign – whether over Shorten's support for Adani, Labor's changes to superannuation, or his mother's biography – tapped into the undiminished distrust the public had for him. It consigned him to the "inside," and darkened his already tarnished image.

But, as Jensen shows, Labor was not playing the game that Morrison was. "Shorten's gamble is that you can replace popularity with policy," writes Jensen.

"If he is right, he upends decades of political orthodoxy. If he is wrong, this may be the last policy election for a generation."

In *The Prosperity Gospel*, Jensen is also taking a gamble. Works of contemporary political history and biography such as this sit within an ever-yawning gulf between the journalism of the day-to-day and the histories that are years in the making. By their greater length, contemporaneousness and flexibility of form, such works allow for more complex and timely discussions about their subjects than might otherwise be available. In doing so, they have the potential to shape enduring perceptions of their subject: think of Alan Reid's wilful John Gorton, Laurie Oakes' grandiose Gough Whitlam, Marr's rage-fuelled Rudd and quixotic Abbott, and Annabel Crabb's mercurial but technocratic Turnbull. In Australia, it should be said, the Quarterly Essay has long worked in this space and provided some of the most acute and significant works of this kind.

But these works come with considerable limitations. They can be hostage to access, captive to views on the "inside"; more often than not, they are prone to all-encompassing character-based narratives, in which participants with tragic flaws or near-magic abilities compete for enduring glories, where personal characteristics are parsed and tied to the national character. Moreover, these works come freighted with the risk that they are out-of-date soon after publication. All biographies have a best-before date, of course – but in the case of works of contemporary biography and history, that date can be as short as that on a carton of milk.

Jensen's gamble with *The Prosperity Gospel*, then, is that people will still go to it for insight. They should. The contrast made in 2019 between Morrison and Shorten might, in 2022, be tried again; Labor might double down on the bet that Shorten made. *The Prosperity Gospel* shows the origins and method of the contrast and the bet. More important, three years on, Morrison will not have the same opportunity to position himself as an outsider. As prime minister, he will have been the ultimate insider for four years – and by that point, the factors that Seldon identified may be much more palpable than they were in 2019. A bad economic headwind could wipe out the Coalition's claims to superior economic management. Support from News Corp could be lost amid the growing static of social media. Inconsistency over policy – whether on climate change, Indigenous affairs, the environment or infrastructure – is hardly out of the realm of possibility. Nor is another bout of instability. By that point, moreover, the Coalition will have been in power for nine years. There might be the feeling that it is time for a change.

Patrick Mullins & Matthew Ricketson

Russell Marks

The title of Erik Jensen's account of the federal election, *The Prosperity Gospel*, is a good one. It captures both Scott Morrison's Pentecostalism and, as Jensen makes clear, the neoliberal faith he asks Australians to retain: work hard, save quietly and you will prosper.

The result of the May 2019 election might suggest that here voters still subscribe to that faith – more so than in, say, the United States or Britain. This election was no Brexitesque collapse of the neoliberal faith. Nor, despite a temptation to draw some neo-fascist bows from Morrison's respect for police and armed forces and from Dutton's win in Dickson, did it return an executive leader who represents the disillusioned. Indeed, Morrison pledged the same miracle Abbott did in 2013: that his government could run and maintain Budget surpluses while decreasing taxes, while paying down public debt and guaranteeing increased funding for services. Roughly the same proportion of voters who bought Abbott's unfulfillable promise to turn straw into gold six years ago bought the same promise this time around. Yet by 2019, the previous six years had been characterised not by Labor's leadership chaos and policy confusion, but by the Coalition's.

The essay's subtitle – *How Scott Morrison Won and Bill Shorten Lost* – promises an explanation for this outcome, but Jensen never really expands beyond what is mostly a literary answer. There's a strong tendency in political journalism to focus too much on agents and not enough on structures. This leads to literary attempts to match leaders' characters to the nation's and to find in the intersections reasons why publics endorse one leader and not another. The best of these exercises use a bit of armchair psychoanalysis – which might explain, say, Rudd's anger or Abbott's stiffness – to lend depth and narrative plausibility. And Jensen is excellent on character. He presents Morrison as securely attached, comfortable in himself and on stage, and Shorten as far less sure of himself, the child of an emotionally absent, alcoholic father and who bonded too urgently with his mother. Jensen concludes that, faced with the choice between them, the insecure nation "has found comfort once again in a hardman who says everything is simple and some of you will be okay."

And perhaps that is enough. The shocking truth of Australian elections is that they are now decided by a swinging middle of chronically disengaged voters who drag themselves to polling booths in a quirk of the compulsory ballot without knowing much at all about who's promising what or how things are going. A large but diminishing majority of voters are still "rusted on" to one party or another: many of these are also relatively disengaged, but they'd never change their vote, so it hardly matters. There are some who change votes between elections yet stay engaged. But there's another 10 per cent whose votes are up for grabs yet for whom politics is background noise, presented through the news bulletins on commercial radio or between evening TV shows – assuming they haven't switched to Spotify and Netflix and can avoid ads almost entirely. Not much is known about how these voters form their intentions, but available evidence suggests they pick up a vibe, almost through osmosis. It's not too far-fetched to imagine them forming preferences based on snatched grabs of leaders on the telly. One seems to talk straight and appears self-assured. The other looks nervous and edgy in an ill-fitting suit. Choice made.

But this kind of analysis misses the deep structures operating through Australia's political and electoral systems. It risks missing asking why so many still seem rusted on to the "prosperity gospel" despite available evidence demonstrating that the gospel's real promise is the transfer of wealth to an already wealthy minority. It risks missing asking why so many blue-collar workers, once Labor's heartland, have become rusted-on Coalition voters.

The role of News Corp, for instance, can't be overstated. Its tabloids are purchased and at least scanned by nearly two million people every day. Their editorial lines, which run through their news coverage, have done more than perhaps anything else to generate and sustain a commonsense conservative liberal disposition in the Australian political culture. *The Australian* and Sky News, purchased by Murdoch in December 2016, provide conservative political leaders with their intellectual energy. In these tasks, able support is provided by Macquarie Radio and magazines like *Spectator Australia* and *Quadrant*, but News has led this resurgence. Anyone who doubts the level of influence Murdoch has had in Australia's political culture should compare this nation to New Zealand, where Murdoch owns no major TV station and no major newspaper, and where Jacinda Ardern provided a model of leadership following the Christchurch massacre that no longer seems possible here. Or the United States, where Murdoch's Fox News has disrupted the political culture to distortion since the channel was launched in 1996. Or that other foreign country, Australia of the 1970s, where a Whitlam government was possible (if only briefly, and then only really with the support of Rupert Murdoch, while it lasted).

Politics is entirely mediated; the medium becomes the message (and the massage, in Marshall McLuhan's later formulation). Any underlying anxiety about the steady transfer of wealth from have-nots to haves is soothed by the constant expressions of neoliberal faith across Murdoch's heavily concentrated outlets. Any head rising above the left-liberal parapet to present an alternative narrative to Morrison's "quiet Australians" is quickly and viciously blown off by Murdoch's attentive and militant opinion army, ever ready to assist capital's objectives by converting them into everyman common sense. Intensively lobbied parliamentarians have, over the decades, created the regulatory environment in which Murdoch's army of influence can rally and prosper.

Jensen makes brief observations about structure: a page on News (recounting Shorten's infamous refusal to meet Murdoch in New York and then the News Corp reaction); snippets on the backdrop Adani provided to this election, especially in Queensland; two mentions of Clive Palmer's extraordinary spend. That there's not more was dictated largely by the essay's research design: like most of Australia's political journalists, Jensen was kept busy following the leaders around the country. He does better than most with the material he gathers – he has a wonderful ability to capture character and mood and feel – but in the end there's a sense this "campaign bus" reporting distracts from the main game.

The biggest bewilderment of election night – how the published polls got it so wrong – has largely been answered. In an age of disengagement, and vanishing landlines, the polling companies' extrapolations have become too problematic. It would have been more honest for the polls to have reported results like 45–43 (with 12 per cent undecided); that's less valuable for the companies, but because it's concomitantly less stimulating for readers it could have meant political journalists returned to the game of generating better analysis and asking better questions.

Because there are still some very important questions which haven't been answered. How did Labor convince itself that running a big-target "policy" campaign, à la Fightback '93, was a good idea? Why has the party still failed to adopt a theory of power and change that would predict, account for and overcome the inevitable pushback by capital and the influence of News Corp? And what explains the consistent ability of the interests of mining capital to defeat those of its farming and tourism competitors? These questions weren't in Jensen's brief. More's the pity. He's an outstanding journalist.

Russell Marks

Response to Correspondence

Erik Jensen

In his first major speech as prime minister, Scott Morrison distinguished between fairness and envy. At the time the words seemed inconsequential. Of Morrison's many skills, one is hiding insights in ordinariness.

"We don't get anywhere by trying to say, 'Well, it's all their fault, it's their fault ...' 'We bring them down, I can go up,'" he said. "That's not fairness in Australia. That's just ugly envy. And I have no truck with that whatsoever. I want to see all Australians succeed, and none at the expense of another. That's an important value."

His framing was mateship. Help was there, but only for the people you knew. He said: "We've got to look after our mates. That's what I believe." And: "As Australians, we look after our mates." And again, just in case: "Remember, my value is: we look after our mates."

More than anything, the last election was about the lie at the middle of the Australian character: that this is a country built on fairness. Morrison understood it to be a lie and he won the election exploiting that. Bill Shorten did not and he lost.

From the outset, Morrison's fairness was contingent. This is what he meant when he promised "a fair go for people who have a go." It's what he meant when he said you don't take from one person to give to another. "It's not about everybody getting the same thing. If you put in, you get to take out, and you get to keep more of what you earn."

Morrison spent the election talking to one half of the country. He said their greed was honest and good, and if they preferred he would call it aspiration. He recast this as fairness for those who worked at it. When Morrison said "all Australians," he said it with the numbers in mind: he was talking to the deserving rich, and there are just enough of them to win elections.

The other part of this is the fear of envy. Envy is the great sin in Australian politics. The fear of it keeps in place a system where the rich cannot be criticised.

To ask for more is to risk the embarrassment of being called resentful. That was the threat Morrison made when he warned of the difference between fairness and envy. Shorten couldn't grasp this and his optimism was called "class war." The people being called envious, however, are in fact the working poor.

Before the election was called, I asked Shorten what he thought the campaign would be about. He answered quickly, to be sure there would be a silence before the next question: "Hope versus fear."

He said this was about his view of society. "This society works best when we're all included. And all Australians are included. When it's not a society run just in the interests of the people who are already powerful."

He spoke as if the word "hope" were a running stitch, the needle of it punching up through the fabric: "I hope that we can reduce inequality. I hope that women can be treated equally. I hope that we can act on climate change, hope that we can afford to see the doctor, hope that our family will grow up safe, hope that we'll have a more independent Australian identity. Hope that I can get people working together more than they currently do. Hope we can kill off the toxic politics of destruction."

Shorten put a piece of chicken in his cheek and continued talking. The meat pulled his mouth upwards into a fearful smile. "I know what you can get done," he said. "This government doesn't deserve another three years."

Morrison has already remade the country, we just haven't noticed yet. His tax cuts will destroy the revenue base that made social welfare possible. Billions of dollars a year will be needed in savings. The stability born of our health and education systems will be lost to lower taxes for the rich.

Labor waved it through. Politicians spend careers looking for reasons not to be brave and this election was a boon for cowardice. The lessons drawn from the loss are already the wrong ones: a blank slate on policy, a sensitivity about assessing wealth. Anthony Albanese says he doesn't believe $200,000 a year makes someone rich.

Morrison's campaign was more sophisticated than Shorten's, if you can use that word to mean its opposite. He made a virtue of simplicity. He tested his messages and stuck to them. He counted each day and kept track of any he lost.

Shorten was less disciplined. He campaigned to govern and Morrison campaigned to win. Shorten believed in the country's desire for fairness. He was in a history lesson when he decided he would like to be prime minister, and his vision of the country is like a teenager's essay on values.

Morrison is a skilled politician, more so than even his party appreciated. Like Howard, he understands the worst of Australia and knows how to make success from it. Bill Shorten is still telling people he won the debates.

Erik Jensen

Judith Brett is emeritus professor of politics at La Trobe University. She is the author of several books, including *Robert Menzies' Forgotten People*, *The Enigmatic Mr Deakin* and *From Secret Ballot to Democracy Sausage*.

Annabel Crabb is the ABC's chief online political writer. Her books include *Losing It*, *Rise of the Ruddbot*, *The Wife Drought* and the Quarterly Essay *Stop at Nothing: The Life and Adventures of Malcolm Turnbull*, which won a 2009 Walkley Award.

Elizabeth Flux is an award-winning writer and editor whose essays and feature articles have been published in *The Saturday Paper*, *The Guardian*, *Island* and others.

Erik Jensen is the award-winning author of *Acute Misfortune* and *On Kate Jennings*. He is founding editor of *The Saturday Paper* and editor-in-chief of Schwartz Media.

Barry Jones joined the ALP in 1950. He served in the Victorian and Australian parliaments, was Minister for Science under Bob Hawke from 1983 to 1990, was ALP National President twice, represented Australia at UNESCO, and is the author of *Sleepers, Wake!* and ten other books.

Kristina Keneally is a Labor senator for New South Wales and a Catholic. She holds a Master of Arts in Catholic theology.

Russell Marks is a lawyer and an honorary research associate at La Trobe University. He is the author of *Crime and Punishment: Offenders and Victims in a Broken Justice System*.

David Marr is the author of *Patrick White: A Life*, *Panic*, *The High Price of Heaven* and *Dark Victory* (with Marian Wilkinson). He has written for *The Sydney Morning Herald*, *The Age*, *The Saturday Paper*, *The Guardian* and *The Monthly*, and been editor of the *National Times*, a reporter for *Four Corners* and presenter of ABC TV's *Media Watch*. He is the author of six bestselling Quarterly Essays.

Patrick Mullins is a Canberra-based academic. *Tiberius with a Telephone*, his biography of the former prime minister Billy McMahon, was published in 2018.

James Newton was Bill Shorten's speechwriter on the 2019 election campaign.

Matthew Ricketson is Professor of Communication at Deakin University. He is the author of three books and editor of two, including *Best Australian Profile*.

QUARTERLY ESSAY
BACK ISSUES

BACK ISSUES: (Prices include GST, postage and handling within Australia.) *Grey indicates out of stock.*

☐ **QE 1** ($15.99) Robert Manne *In Denial*
☐ **QE 2** ($15.99) John Birmingham *Appeasing Jakarta*
☐ **QE 3** ($15.99) Guy Rundle *The Opportunist*
☐ **QE 4** ($15.99) Don Watson *Rabbit Syndrome*
☐ **QE 5** ($15.99) Mungo MacCallum *Girt By Sea*
☐ **QE 6** ($15.99) John Button *Beyond Belief*
☐ **QE 7** ($15.99) John Martinkus *Paradise Betrayed*
☐ **QE 8** ($15.99) Amanda Lohrey *Groundswell*
☐ **QE 9** ($15.99) Tim Flannery *Beautiful Lies*
☐ **QE 10** ($15.99) Gideon Haigh *Bad Company*
☐ **QE 11** ($15.99) Germaine Greer *Whitefella Jump Up*
☐ **QE 12** ($15.99) David Malouf *Made in England*
☐ **QE 13** ($15.99) Robert Manne with David Corlett *Sending Them Home*
☐ **QE 14** ($15.99) Paul McGeough *Mission Impossible*
☐ **QE 15** ($15.99) Margaret Simons *Latham's World*
☐ **QE 16** ($15.99) Raimond Gaita *Breach of Trust*
☐ **QE 17** ($15.99) John Hirst *'Kangaroo Court'*
☐ **QE 18** ($15.99) Gail Bell *The Worried Well*
☐ **QE 19** ($15.99) Judith Brett *Relaxed & Comfortable*
☐ **QE 20** ($15.99) John Birmingham *A Time for War*
☐ **QE 21** ($15.99) Clive Hamilton *What's Left?*
☐ **QE 22** ($15.99) Amanda Lohrey *Voting for Jesus*
☐ **QE 23** ($15.99) Inga Clendinnen *The History Question*
☐ **QE 24** ($15.99) Robyn Davidson *No Fixed Address*
☐ **QE 25** ($15.99) Peter Hartcher *Bipolar Nation*
☐ **QE 26** ($15.99) David Marr *His Master's Voice*
☐ **QE 27** ($15.99) Ian Lowe *Reaction Time*
☐ **QE 28** ($15.99) Judith Brett *Exit Right*
☐ **QE 29** ($15.99) Anne Manne *Love & Money*
☐ **QE 30** ($15.99) Paul Toohey *Last Drinks*
☐ **QE 31** ($15.99) Tim Flannery *Now or Never*
☐ **QE 32** ($15.99) Kate Jennings *American Revolution*
☐ **QE 33** ($15.99) Guy Pearse *Quarry Vision*
☐ **QE 34** ($15.99) Annabel Crabb *Stop at Nothing*
☐ **QE 35** ($15.99) Noel Pearson *Radical Hope*
☐ **QE 36** ($15.99) Mungo MacCallum *Australian Story*
☐ **QE 37** ($15.99) Waleed Aly *What's Right?*

☐ **QE 38** ($15.99) David Marr *Power Trip*
☐ **QE 39** ($15.99) Hugh White *Power Shift*
☐ **QE 40** ($15.99) George Megalogenis *Trivial Pursuit*
☐ **QE 41** ($15.99) David Malouf *The Happy Life*
☐ **QE 42** ($15.99) Judith Brett *Fair Share*
☐ **QE 43** ($15.99) Robert Manne *Bad News*
☐ **QE 44** ($15.99) Andrew Charlton *Man-Made World*
☐ **QE 45** ($15.99) Anna Krien *Us and Them*
☐ **QE 46** ($15.99) Laura Tingle *Great Expectations*
☐ **QE 47** ($15.99) David Marr *Political Animal*
☐ **QE 48** ($15.99) Tim Flannery *After the Future*
☐ **QE 49** ($15.99) Mark Latham *Not Dead Yet*
☐ **QE 50** ($15.99) Anna Goldsworthy *Unfinished Business*
☐ **QE 51** ($15.99) David Marr *The Prince*
☐ **QE 52** ($15.99) Linda Jaivin *Found in Translation*
☐ **QE 53** ($15.99) Paul Toohey *That Sinking Feeling*
☐ **QE 54** ($15.99) Andrew Charlton *Dragon's Tail*
☐ **QE 55** ($15.99) Noel Pearson *A Rightful Place*
☐ **QE 56** ($15.99) Guy Rundle *Clivosaurus*
☐ **QE 57** ($15.99) Karen Hitchcock *Dear Life*
☐ **QE 58** ($15.99) David Kilcullen *Blood Year*
☐ **QE 59** ($15.99) David Marr *Faction Man*
☐ **QE 60** ($15.99) Laura Tingle *Political Amnesia*
☐ **QE 61** ($15.99) George Megalogenis *Balancing Act*
☐ **QE 62** ($15.99) James Brown *Firing Line*
☐ **QE 63** ($15.99) Don Watson *Enemy Within*
☐ **QE 64** ($15.99) Stan Grant *The Australian Dream*
☐ **QE 65** ($15.99) David Marr *The White Queen*
☐ **QE 66** ($15.99) Anna Krien *The Long Goodbye*
☐ **QE 67** ($15.99) Benjamin Law *Moral Panic 101*
☐ **QE 68** ($15.99) Hugh White *Without America*
☐ **QE 69** ($15.99) Mark McKenna *Moment of Truth*
☐ **QE 70** ($15.99) Richard Denniss *Dead Right*
☐ **QE 71** ($15.99) Laura Tingle *Follow the Leader*
☐ **QE 72** ($22.99) Sebastian Smee *Net Loss*
☐ **QE 73** ($22.99) Rebecca Huntley *Australia Fair*
☐ **QE 74** ($22.99) Erik Jensen *The Prosperity Gospel*

NAME:

ADDRESS:

EMAIL: PHONE:

Please include this form with payment details overleaf.

☐ **ONE-YEAR AUTO-RENEWING PRINT AND DIGITAL SUBSCRIPTION:** $69.95*
REQUIRES EMAIL, 4 issues, save 24% off the cover price

☐ **TWO-YEAR PRINT AND DIGITAL SUBSCRIPTION:** $149.95 8 issues

☐ **ONE-YEAR AUTO-RENEWING PRINT AND DIGITAL INTERNATIONAL SUBSCRIPTION:** $109.95*
REQUIRES EMAIL, 4 issues

☐ **ONE-YEAR DIGITAL ONLY SUBSCRIPTION:** $49.95 4 issues

☐ **ONE-YEAR PRINT AND DIGITAL GIFT SUBSCRIPTION:** $79.95 4 issues, save 13% off the cover
price. Subscriptions outside Australia **$119.95**

☐ **TWO-YEAR PRINT AND DIGITAL GIFT SUBSCRIPTION** $149.95 8 issues, save 13% off the cover
price

☐ TICK HERE TO COMMENCE SUBSCRIPTION WITH THE CURRENT ISSUE

SUBSCRIBER'S NAME:

ADDRESS:

EMAIL: PHONE:

RECIPIENT'S NAME:

ADDRESS:

EMAIL: PHONE:

PAYMENT DETAILS: Enclose a cheque/money order made out to Schwartz Books Pty Ltd.
Or debit my credit card (MasterCard, Visa and Amex accepted).
Freepost: Quarterly Essay, Reply Paid 90094, Carlton VIC 3053
All prices include GST, postage and handling.

CARD NO. ☐☐☐☐ ☐☐☐☐ ☐☐☐☐ ☐☐☐☐

EXPIRY DATE: /   CCV: AMOUNT: $

PURCHASER'S NAME: SIGNATURE:

PURCHASER'S EMAIL:

Subscribe online at **quarterlyessay.com/subscribe** • Freecall: 1800 077 514 • Phone: 03 9486 0288
Email: subscribe@quarterlyessay.com (please do not send electronic scans of this form)

* Your subscription will automatically renew until you notify us to stop. Prior to the end of your subscription period, we will
  send you a reminder notice that will indicate the renewal price. If you do not notify us to stop the renewal, your credit or debit
  card will automatically be charged for the same period. You may notify us to stop the renewal via the account dashboard or by
  contacting us. Australian subscriptions only.